MW00899781

CHASING HORIZONS

GABY'S STORY

By

HILLREY A DUFNER

Library of Congress Control Number: 2013906575
CreateSpace Independent Publishing Platform
North Charleston, South Carolina

Forward

I started and stopped writing this book many times over a period of a dozen years. I published two other novels and two children's books between beginning this effort and its completion. Though the writing of the book was very difficult for me, it is the result of an internal drive and a love I could not squelch. The story is too important to not share, but so very close and personal that sharing it is a daunting task.

There are times in most people's lives when they find themselves connected with very special people. This is especially true of professional educators such as me. In my professional life, I have met some very bright and very determined students, some students whose talents were overshadowed by their dedication, and many, many students whose memorable characteristics are that they are very good people. There are many I have worked with that were very difficult. I have loved them all. I have had a positive impact on some students and helped change a few lives for the better and, I pray, caused little damage. Most students have had great impact on my life and helped me grow into a better person. I have been inspired by too many of several thousands of students over my thirty-nine years as an educator to mention by name. This book could have been about any one of a large number of former students who have taught me great lessons.

The student this book is about, I never had in a class, but she inspired me because of her perseverance, her courage, and her clear vision of a future most people would have said was impossible for her. Gaby grew up in Mexico to the age of eleven then came to the United States the daughter of a poor immigrant farm-worker. She had few and small prospects and many obstacles to overcome, but through her accomplishments, she has lived the definition of what it means to be an American with a dream.

When I first met Gaby, I knew she was especially bright, but I had no idea how gritty and courageous she was until she convinced me to help her realize a small part of her larger dream. Her story of a dream accomplished in the face of detractors, overwhelming tragedy, and serious injury will inspire every adolescent girl and boy that cannot yet see a good future for themselves, and by every man and woman who has given up on a dream. Gaby clearly demonstrated that the impossible is achieved by those who attempt the impossible.

This book is dedicated to: **Sanjuanita Garces de Garza,** *Gabriela's mother, for her dedicated efforts at being a wise, caring, and loving mother to her children and grandchild. She is a loving and forgiving wife, mother, and friend beyond all reasonable human expectation.*

And in memory of **El Profesor Jose Jaime Vargas,** *the quiet, dedicated, and courageous teacher who gave up higher pay and greater prestige to spend his teaching career with the children of Ejido Buena Vista, a poor village in northern Mexico. The children could never repay him, but without him they would never have been as successful. They will never forget his dedication, his patience, his kindness, his example, or his teachings.*

1

First Pains

The sky was a heavy gray as it hung over the rain-soaked and muddy plains of Northern Mexico in the winter of 1978. Dark clouds hid the early morning moon and sullenly held the promise of more frigid rain. In the gentle but biting breeze, bare tree limbs clawed like thin, gnarled, misshapen fingers over a small wooden house in the dark wee hours of the early winter morning. A dim light shone from the drafty kitchen where Mrs. Garza winced and stood still for a moment, pain showing in her face as yet another constriction told of her third child to be born that day. On November 7, 1978, in the small tightly-designed ejido (village) called Buena Vista, situated fourteen miles from the city of Reynosa, Tamaulipas, Mrs. Garza had awakened at three-fifteen in the morning to the onset of childbirth. She had a primal urge to move about that she could not deny, but still she did not wish to awaken her husband, snoring softly and sleeping soundly in their bed, so she moved quietly.

The biting cold outside slipped freely inside the house, penetrating through cracks in the walls, under doors, and around windows. The frigid air also soaked almost unimpeded through the thin, wet planks that formed the walls of the house, chilling any occupant who slipped from beneath the bed covers. Mrs. Garza moved gingerly and quietly around the kitchen preparing coffee. Gentle groans escaped her lips occasionally as the baby offered her sudden and mildly painful reminders of her condition. The pains seemed normal to her, and Mrs. Garza took comfort in the normalcy, but she could not help but remember on this day what had happened to her first child. She shivered involuntarily as the unwelcome thought worried the edges of her consciousness then broke fully into her thinking. The child she carried this day was a girl. Mrs. Garza, formerly Sanjuanita Garces Trevino, was comfortable in the knowledge that the baby was a girl. A girl is what she prayed for. She had faith that God had heard her and would grant her request. Sanjuanita was brought up to believe that God answers prayers, and since her prayers for boys had been answered twice, she was confident her prayers for a girl would be granted also.

The Garza family home was one of eighteen small wooden-frame houses built mostly from second-hand lumber and stucco in the rural village that sat in the state of Tamaulipas, Mexico, five kilometers outside Ciudad Rio Bravo. Mrs. Garza had another child, Gilberto, now four years old. Mrs. Garza had known Gilberto was a boy long before he was born, because when she was expecting him, she had prayed for a boy. But the boy she now enjoyed was not her first child. There was another baby she had carried a year before Gilberto, Jr. was born. The pains she had endured with that first child were still worrying her mind. Because of this memory that continued to periodically intrude on her peace, she was anxious and a little frightened for her baby girl not yet born.

She had been twenty-two years old and married only one month in April of 1973, when the first pains came that she now recalled being associated with birth. The first pains were not hurts to her body. Sanjuanita had been ignorant of the ways of men, women, and life, and she had always been a shy, private person who was easily embarrassed by being pushed into the public eye. That day her ignorance caused her to be the object of much poking of fun. She was not accustomed to being the target of teasing, and she hated it.

At a large family gathering, Sanjuanita complained to her mother that she was feeling very ill every morning lately and had missed her monthly flow. On this November morning as she prepared to welcome her first daughter, she recalled the humiliation she had felt when her mother laughed at her ignorance in the midst of a kitchen full of women relatives. It had hurt no less than if she had been slapped by her own mother, and she had wanted to run away but could not. One just did not run away from family. Later she could see that it was simply an older woman having some gentle fun at the expense of a younger woman in her ignorance. She realized her mother had in fact been very joy-filled, celebrating the news of a grand-child, and that joy had caused the reaction that Sanjuanita found so hurtful; her mother had been completely unaware that she hurt her daughter. The grandmother-to-be had giggled as she told Sanjuanita that without doubt she was pregnant with her first child. On this November morning, she had long since come to peace with the incident and forgiven everyone, but the memory still was painful. Trying to shake it from her mind, Sanjuanita busied herself in the kitchen, but her face stung afresh as she recalled the embarrassment. Another more painful memory gave her a sense of dread that she tried unsuccessfully to put away.

When she married, Sanjuanita had known almost nothing of pregnan-cy. She was born the youngest of eight children on a remote ranch in rural Mexico and had been 'protected' from such knowledge. As the youngest in a family largely isolated from the world, she had never watched her mother or any woman develop with child, and she had never witnessed a birth. She was not told of marriage matters. Because she was so shy, even with her family, she had not broken the silence to ask about that which 'nice' girls should not know. Sanjuanita was even sheltered from caring for the live-stock, from which she could have learned some of the things of life.

In spite of her obvious discomfort, Sanjuanita's family was thrilled that she was pregnant. Sanjuanita was glad they were happy, but afraid of all the things she didn't know and at a loss of where to learn them. Even after all the congratulations and celebration for the new life to be welcomed into the family, Sanjuanita still did not know what to expect from this new turn of events. Over the next few weeks, Sanjuanita's mother occasionally of-fered belated assistance and gave considerable advice in hopes of teaching her the things she would need to know

Gilberto Garza, "Beto," Sanjuanita's husband, had been emotionally distancing himself from her since the day after their wedding night. He lived at their meager home, and spent his time during the day working the fields, his evenings were spent away from his new bride. Beto came into their small house in the evenings, washed off the dirt of the day's work, and dressed to go out by himself. In the heavy silence of things hidden and unspoken, he ate the suppers Sanjuanita prepared, then left to spend his nights with friends. Often he was in the bars dancing with other women all night, returning only in time to eat another meal Sanjuanita would prepare then begin a new day's work. Sanjuanita stayed at home waiting for him, alone and uninvited to his evenings out. She patiently waited for her child to be born. In public, and even to her husband, she smiled bravely so none would know of her unhappiness, but at home alone at night, in the darkness, she was lonely and sad and afraid, and heart broken. Sanjuanita wept night after night as her feelings and her body changed with pregnancy. Nothing seemed to go as it should and certainly not as she had dreamed.

Sanjuanita took care of their small holdings and tried to create profits from the little they had. Each morning she was up before dawn, cooking breakfast for her new husband. Later in the morning, she would begin preparing his lunch. When the food was ready, she walked to the fields to deliver the meal. In the afternoon, shortly before dark, Sanjuanita began cooking supper for her husband. Between her cooking responsibilities, she cared for the stock they had been given as wedding gifts. She fed the cow, milked her, and turned her and the calf out to graze.

Part of the milk she set aside, allowing the cream to rise to the top and be skimmed off for making butter, some to use and some to sell. Some of the milk she used for making cheese, both to eat and sell at market alongside the butter. In addition, she took care of a small garden and gathered produce to sell on market days. Of course, throughout the day, in the minutes between her other tasks, Sanjuanita cleaned and scrubbed the small house.

After a short time, Gilberto added to her burdens. Her husband brought an infant boy for her to care for each day. He did not tell her where the child came from or whose he was. In spite of all the hard work, sorrow, and worry, her pregnancy went well. Shortly before her first baby was to be born, Sanjuanita's husband admitted that the child he brought for her to babysit was his child by another woman. There was no payment for her efforts, and even in the face of this news and her silent heartbreak and sadness, she continued caring for the child without complaint. She did not fault the child and cared for him as well as she hoped someone would care for her children if she could not.

It was on December 31, 1973, that Sanjuanita first began to suffer from pains that caused her concern. She did not know what was happening, but her intuition told her that something was wrong; it did not feel right. Several women had told her what it would feel like to birth a child. She was alarmed by the strangeness of events that she had not been warned about. Her few advisors had told her that there would be great pain, but neglected to tell her of the location of the pain or of its duration, as well as the meaning of greater frequency or intensity. Later she realized the pains she felt on that New Year's Eve had been early-birth contractions.

Luckily Gilberto was at home when the pains began. He decided to take her to Reynosa to the hospital. Later, at the busy hospital, the doctor examined her briefly, gave her an injection for the pain, and proclaimed her not yet ready to deliver. They went back home to the three acres they lived on and their small one-room home to celebrate the New Year with friends. Shortly the pains stopped, and Sanjuanita felt different; not better but not a lot worse. However, she was now constantly afraid for her child. In spite of this anxiety, she joined the other women of the ejido in cooking and other preparations for the New Year's fiesta. By the next morning, January 1, 1974, Sanjuanita began noticing a progressive difference in the child she carried. By the end of the sixth day after the doctor had given her the injection for pain, her baby no longer kicked, and when Sanjuanita moved, it felt as if she were carrying a heavy ball in a sack in her stomach. She asked to be taken back to the doctor. Gilberto reluctantly and angrily drove her over the rough roads back to the hospital in Reynosa. Shortly after the doctor examined her, he gave the young couple the sad news that their child had died. Gilberto was stoic and accepted the news without a word, but Sanjuanita was heartbroken. The loss of her first child created a new set of fears she would carry throughout her child-bearing years.

2

Gabriela: The Birth

ilberto, Sanjuanita's second child survived. He was born in June of 1975 after a very successful and uneventful pregnancy with no complications, and the delivery was easy and fast. Although Sanjuanita had worried all through the pregnancy, Gilberto was born healthy and robust. However, on this early November morning before dawn and the birth of her third child, she still had some small but sharply-ominous feelings in her stomach and in her mind. Feelings pushed themselves on her in sequence; the queasiness one experiences during the plunge of a steep rollercoaster hit her first, quickly followed by the dread felt as one begins to climb again. Those feelings mixed with the expectation in her mind that in the end, after the pain and worry, her daughter would be fine. In this early morning, while her husband and little boy slept, Sanjuanita wept quietly as she earnestly prayed to God for her child. Her prayers finished, she drank her coffee and began methodically making preparations to birth a little girl.

Shortly after daybreak, as the eastern horizon shone brightly but before the sun peeked over the edge of the earth, Sanjuanita quietly shook her husband. Beto grumbled at the news that his daughter was soon to be born, but rose and began his morning stirring. It was even colder now that the sun was coming up. The air outside was laden with moisture. Beto went to work hauling what belongings they would need for the day. He loaded his old flatbed Ford truck with blankets, coats, clean clothes, and the meager baby-girl trappings Sanjuanita had collected and made. The unpaved road was rutted and muddy from recent rains, so they had to take the big truck; Gilberto feared the smaller pickup would get stuck in a pothole or rut. Gilberto Junior was awakened and dressed after the truck was running and the cab warm. Beto wrapped the sleepy child in a blanket and loaded him into the cab of the truck between the two adults. Sanjuanita's pains had been coming at regular intervals, but they stopped abruptly as the family was about to leave the house, so they decided to wait a while. Shortly after two in the afternoon, the pains began again in earnest, and soon young Gilberto was in the truck again, bouncing along the rough, muddy, road between his parents, traveling the highway leading to Rio Bravo and the hospital.

Weeks before that day, Beto had made plans to go to the races in Matamoros that very afternoon. He loved racing his purple Dodge Charger and often won money. He derived great enjoyment from the feeling of power and speed produced by the four-hundred-plus horsepower engine. He refused to change his plans because of the impending birth of his daughter. With the race at the forefront of his mind, and realizing he could make it in time for the start if he hurried, he dropped Sanjuanita and Gilberto Junior off at the front door of the hospital before returning home to get his purple Dodge Charger. Soon he was driving his racing car out the muddy entrance of their ejido, heading for Matamoros, a few miles east of Rio Bravo and about two miles on the Mexico side of the border between Mexico and Texas. While Beto was at the races, his daughter was born. She was perfect. She had a full head of coal-black hair, dark eyes, and round cheeks. Sanjuanita named her Gabriela, and almost immediately she became 'Gaby.'

Gabriela's first visitor at the hospital was a friend of her mother's family. Years later, Gabriela would still not be able to speak his name, but he would brag to her at every opportunity that, besides her mother, he was the first to kiss her. Sanjuanita's family came to see her in the hospital that same evening as soon as they could get away from their chores. Sanjuanita, her family, and Gilberto Junior celebrated the new family member. They took turns holding her and telling her how beautiful she was and how much they were going to care for her. After seeing the new baby girl, one of Sanjuanita's brothers went to find Gilberto at the races to tell him his daughter had been born. He bragged to the new father that she was a gorgeous seven pounds and nineteen inches long. He talked about her long hair and fat cheeks. Having received the news, Gilberto responded, "Great. I'll stop by in a while."

Years later, in 1983, another boy, Gamaliel, was born into the family. And finally in 1989 another boy, German, was born, thus completing the Garza family. Gabriela nicknamed German "Casper" after the cartoon ghost, because as soon as he was old enough to walk, he quietly followed her everywhere she went. There were times he seemed to have walked through a closed door or a wall, appearing unexpectedly at her side. He always seemed to be happy being close to his big sister.

3

Ejido Buena Vista

Ejido Buena Vista, roughly translated to "The Beautiful Panorama," was built on a plot of land subdivided into many smaller lots. Each residential lot in the ejido was sold with a matching plot of farmland nearby. In Mexico, an ejido was a village built on land expropriated from large private landowners and redistributed for Use as communal farmland, especially to marginal populations. People who moved into ejidos were usually the very poor who bought or were given a place to build a home and land close by from which to make a living. The Mexican government set up this design in order to encourage better agricultural production to feed the country. The original design and function of ejidos were generally not honored beyond the first generation; free enterprise has a tendency of taking over good intentions.

Abuelo Pablo, Gilberto's father, was lucky enough to live during the time of the distribution, and to be offered land by the Mexican Government.

He promised to use the land to produce food crops. Pablo Garza Guzman made his promise and asked for fourteen hectares, about twenty-eight acres. His request was granted. He received the land and an unimproved lot in the nearby unpopulated Ejido Buena Vista. He chose to build a house of mud and grass on the farm plot he named El Rancho Las Maravillas (The Wonderful Ranch), where he was to live. He later built a small frame house in Buena Vista to satisfy his wife.

When Abuelo Pablo got old and so feeble he was unable to farm the land, Gilberto took over his father's house in Ejido Buena Vista and worked the land. Abuelo Pablo remained in his mud-hut on the ranch. Gilberto prospered and soon began buying plots of land from those who left the ejido, needed money, or had to sell because of a family emergency or other financial crisis. He bought in such a way to land-lock parcels of land. Mexico had no laws that allow an owner to demand a right-of-way or free access to his land. The owner of landlocked property also has no right to cross someone else's property in order to enter his own property. The owner of land surrounded by the properties of others would not be able to get his equipment in to farm the parcel, or even legally visit his property without the goodwill of the owners of the surrounding parcels of land.

After purchasing land around a plot and successfully locking it in, Gilberto would deny the owner of the plot access and begin the process of negotiating to buy the land at a much reduced price. He could get very good deals as landlocked property was Useless to the owner and could not be easily sold to anyone who did not also own some of the surrounding land. If the landlocked property was surrounded by more than one person, there was a better chance of getting a reasonable settlement. If the owner of the landlocked parcel could get two bidders emotionally involved in winning the bid, he might even make a profit. If Gilberto found himself bidding against another landowner, he remained aware of the situation and would not allow himself to get emotionally involved. Instead, he would bid up the price then, when the bid was higher than the value of the property, he would acquiesce, thereby punishing anyone who bid against him. He seldom lost this chess match. By the year 1990, Gilberto owned and farmed a very large parcel of land, much more than his father had left him, making him a very successful farmer. However, his finances were very vulnerable to the whims of the market and weather. In those contests, he could not be assured a win.

4

Important People

Every person has important people, conditions, and events in their lives. Parents, grandparents, aunts, uncles, priests, teachers, and even brothers and sisters may help direct and train those who look up to them. Sometimes these influential people perform the training purposefully, and sometimes it happens that they simply lead by example and the trainer is unaware of their effect. Everyone has someone who looks up to, and in some ways emulates, them. On the other hand, most people also have someone in whom they see not something to copy, but something to avoid becoming. Thieves may have honest children. Hurtful people may raise children with kind and tender hearts. Good caring people may have offspring who are arrogant and lacking in character. Everyone learns something from the people with whom they associate. Gabriela had some very influential people in her life that helped her to grow into herself.

Sometimes people are changed and directed by events or conditions that are seemingly unavoidable. A marathoner's life changes when he is involved in a motorcycle accident that crushes the femur of one leg. He becomes bitter and takes his misfortune out on others, or he learns from the experience and directs his passion elsewhere. An epileptic may learn to build her life around the episodes so she can be productive. A man blinded in one eye may learn to balance all over again and to find other ways to judge distance.

Events can be very influential. Men who have been drunkards and scoundrels sober up and become pillars of the community after the birth of a child whom they never want to disappoint. A mild-mannered pillar of the community becomes a mass murderer after witnessing an accidental death and becoming obsessed with reliving, again and again, the experience of watching another human die. People influence each other, often without knowing or intending to influence or to be influenced.

Gabriela has had people, conditions, and events that have touched her life and helped her to become who she is. She gravitated to people who could teach her, and she listened.

GROWING UP WITH PAPI

Gilberto Garza was Gabriela's hero as should be every father of a little girl. From a very young age, she demanded that he spoil her. She demanded he take her with him wherever he went, and whenever practical, he did. At times, even when it wasn't so practical, she would go with him anyway. He found it hard to resist the very strong-willed little girl that adored him.

Ejido Buena Vista was a village steeped in poverty by most standards, but it was not without its sources of entertainment. Rain came seldom, but whenever it did, it was welcomed. During the winter, good rains foretold good crops, and good crops meant everyone could afford a little extra in the form of better food, new clothing, additions to houses, and more frequent trips to town for various treats. During the late spring through the early fall, a good rain usually brought enough water to fill the irrigation canal that ran through the area's farms.

While the Garza family lived there, a full canal meant water for crops to the farmers and water deep enough for swimming to children in the ejido. The children would gather at the deepest hole and frolic in the water until their skin wrinkled or they got so cold they had to get out. During the infrequent rainy periods, everyone learned to swim and swam every chance they got as long as the water lasted. When the water was almost all used or evaporated, children would have a great time wallowing in the mud until they were forbidden to go back by weary parents.

The older boys and grown men had their entertainment in a downpour also. During a good rain, Gilberto would take his flatbed truck and any number of ejido men and boys to go mudding. The local men and older boys would load onto the flatbed of the truck, talking and laughing in anticipation of fun and a taste of living on the edge. Beto drove the truck fully loaded with excited men to the low spot in his horse pasture where water would puddle. The soil was a sand and clay mixture that allowed water to soak through it slowly. Rainwater expanded the clay on the surface and sealed it against soaking into the layers below. The wet clay surface would hold water for a long time. As it was raining, the low spot would build up a wide shallow pool of water with a very thin layer of slippery mud. If Beto gained a little speed before hitting the low spot, water shot high on both sides of the truck, encouraging shouts from the men riding on the bed. Some shouts were indicative of excitement, and some were from the shock of being drenched in cold water. The tires on Beto's truck would soon gather so much mud in the treads of the tires they could no longer grip the slick ground. That was when the best fun began. The truck would slide in long unpredictable arcs, splashing water in a huge sprays and waves. Mud would sling off the back tires directly behind the truck. Beto would get the truck moving then jerk the steering wheel to slide the truck sideways or skid in circles, giving everyone an exciting ride until it threw them off into the mud to the delight and derision of everyone else. There were few places on the truck to grab and hold on to, so avoiding being slung into the pool was a challenge. Soon after the sliding began, men would be clinging to the truck while running beside it in attempts to get back on. Others would be chasing the truck while slipping and sliding themselves, and a few would be lying in the water, laughing too hard to get up.

Barely out of toddlerhood, Gaby watched the men as they climbed laughing and joking onto the wet bed of her papi's truck in the rain. She knew she would not be invited to ride, so she would run through the rain to the horse pasture fence to watch the fun. She tried many times to get Beto to allow her to ride on the truck bed. The answer was always, "No." or "Maybe next time." As she got older, she became emboldened enough to argue with Beto to ride. Finally, when she was three, he relented far enough to allow her to ride in the cab with him. It wasn't everything she wanted, but it was movement in the right direction, so she took it. As Beto drove in circles, sliding and skidding through the mud and throwing men off, Gaby kneeled on the seat watching through the back window of the cab. She squealed, clapped, jumped, and laughed as the men on the bed tried to stand or sit without falling over or off the truck bed, all the while laughing with each other like small children in a mud puddle. Given the opportunity, a jokester would push someone else off and into the mud. Soon, it was every man for himself. Occasionally a rider would fall off the truck into the mud and drag someone else with him. Everyone still on the truck had a great time laughing at those trying to stand on the slick surface, running to catch the truck and continue their ride. Eventually Beto would stop and let them back on. When one climbed back on the truck, he brought mud with him, eventually making the bed as slick as the mud hole. Soon slipping off became more common than hanging on, and everyone was soaked and muddy and laughing so hard it was difficult for anyone to get up out of the mud much less stay on the truck. Eventually, the men would become so exhausted from the effort that they would simply lie down in the shallow water. Because it looked like so much fun, Gaby often begged to ride on the bed of the truck. Beto never allowed it.

When Beto, who Gaby always called Papi, had to run an errand in Rio Bravo or Reynosa, Gaby was often allowed to go along. If the first answer was no, as it usually was, a demanding stamp of her small foot and the crossing of her little arms across her chest usually brought Papi around to her way of thinking, and he would relent with a wry smile. They normally left early in the morning and had breakfast in town. Occasionally Papi would spend most of the morning shopping for ranch equipment or seed for the spring planting. Those days were exciting and special for Gaby because most of the time, going with Papi into Rio Bravo meant they would also eat lunch in the city. Gaby insisted on the right to choose where they ate lunch. She always chose the same meal. In her young mind, the only acceptable lunch was taquitos and orange soda from "Taqueria Barrilitos" as Gaby called it. The tortillas were fresh, and the salsa was perfect. Taquitos came in orders of six, so she would always get a half order and a bottle of orange soda called Barrilitos which was the brand Gaby nicknamed the store after. For the next hour, she would be busy happily eating her tacos and drinking her soda. On occasion, Papi would get a haircut in the barbershop across the street from her favorite taqueria. Papi would buy her a half order of taquitos and a bottle of orange soda so she could eat in the barbershop while she waited for him to get his haircut. Since he knew the owner of the barbershop, and Gaby was a favorite visitor, she had permission to take her food inside. As she was growing up, Gaby would have rather been with her Papi than anyone else in the world, except maybe her mother.

GROWING UP WITH ABUELITA FELA

Life was good for Gabriela during her young childhood in Ejido Buena Vista. Her father's mother owned and ran one of the two small convenience stores in the area, and her mother's mother, *Abuelita* (Grandmother) Fela, would visit often. On her visits, she arrived on a Friday evening on the train that rolled through Ejido Buena Vista. The train most often had no reason to stop, but on the occasional Friday evening it would make a brief stop to let off passengers or take on new riders.

Sanjuanita's mother was a small woman with a ready smile and a heart full of love for her grandchildren. She held a special place in her heart for Gaby. That happy and loving heart was, however, a very sick heart and under a doctor's care. To complicate matters, Abuelita Fela had a great love for candy, sodas, and other snack foods, which of course the doctors told her she could not eat. On her visits to Ejido Buena Vista and Gaby, she would send Sanjuanita to the fields early in the morning with Gilberto and begin preparing the noon meal herself. Once Gabriela's mother was away from the house, she would go to the bedroom she shared with Gaby, get her purse, take out a little money, and send Gabriela to her paternal grandmother's store for two of anything she wanted. Gaby ran quickly but shopped carefully and negotiated hard with her other grandmother to get the most sweets for the small amount of money she was given. When she returned home, Gabriela would stash the goodies in her room under the bedcovers and pillows. After lunch, while everyone else was taking their midday siesta, grandmother and granddaughter would sneak into Gabriela's room to talk, giggle, and gorge themselves on the sodas and snacks the doctors had forbidden the grandmother to eat.

On one of those days, after the little grandmother and Gaby had settled in to eat the sweets, Sanjuanita rose early from her siesta and heard soft giggles coming from Gaby's room. She tried to go into the room to see what was going on, but the two miscreants had blocked the door with a chair and student desk bought for Gaby's home studies. Sanjuanita could not budge the door. She peered through the small keyhole in the door and knocked. "Mama, Gaby, what are you doing? What is going on in there?"

She got the standard answer. "Nothing! We aren't doing nothing! Just laughing." But Sanjuanita could hear the crinkling of wrappers as the two quickly piled the candy, chips, and sodas under their wide skirts. But more than that, Sanjuanita could hear the giggling which was of the sort young girls emit when they are being naughty.

Sanjuanita yelled through the door, "Yes, you are! I know what you are doing! You are eating food you are not supposed to eat." The more Sanjuanita yelled, the more the pair giggled. After that first day of being discovered, Sanjuanita became an important part of the game. Gaby and grandmother would scheme and plot to secure the food, keep it hidden, and sneak into the room together. They would then wait for quiet before eating to their hearts' content. Sanjuanita provided a great foil to their mischief, accusing, pounding on the door, or storming outside to tap on the window, forcing the pair to hide their booty. For Gaby, it was a wonderful game full of delicious food and equally delicious plotting with grandmother against the wits of her mother, and it was all sprinkled generously with girlish giggling and laughter.

As Abuelita Fela prepared to end her visit, usually on Sunday afternoon, she often put off her departure and enjoyed her visit until the last possible moment. At times she waited a little too long and had to send a grandchild ahead of her to hold the train until she could arrive. She always dressed in her very best and made quite a sight running through the Ejido Buena Vista in her nicest clothes, laughing with Gaby and giggling like a small girl. She always seemed joyful after yet another visit with her daughter's family. She always arrived at the train out of breath, sometimes holding her chest in a futile attempt to relieve pains that she would not complain about.

More than the fun times shared with her, Gaby remembers Abuelita Fela's strong character. She was a determined woman. Abuelita lost her husband in February of 1978, the same year Gaby was born. After the loss of her husband, Abuelita transformed into a new woman. She was not only the leader of her family, but she also had the responsibility of successfully running the acres of ranch her husband and she had acquired over the years.

Abuelita was also very aware that she didn't have many years to live because of her weak heart, but she never mentioned her illness to any of her eight children or many grandchildren. In this way, she avoided their worried questions about her health, a topic not open to discussion. The children knew that her heart was weak, but their frequent questions usually went answered; she was very adept at changing the conversation to something of more interest to her.

After Gaby's first year of school, at age six, her parents would allow her to travel with Abuelita. Gaby clearly remembers the first long trip she took with her abuelita to Monterrey to visit Sanjuanita's sister who lived a few miles away from the metro area. Because Abuelita was getting older and had heart trouble, Sanjuanita worried about them traveling on their own; especially because they were traveling to a strange and busy city. However, Abuelita was determined to make the trip, and she always had the last word in any argument. They took the train from the ejido to Rio Bravo. Abuelita gave Gaby money and allowed her to pay for the ride and choose their seats. Although Gaby had seen the train come through the Ejido Buena Vista all her life, this was her first train ride. It was exciting to see all the trees pass by in front other at such a great speed. She kept pointing to the trees and telling Abuelita Fela how happy she was to be with her. Gaby could tell the train ride was nothing new for Abuelita, because she was not nearly as excited as Gaby was. The ride to Rio Bravo was about twenty minutes, and the train dropped them off a few blocks from the bus terminal from which they would take a bus all the way to Monterrey, several hours away. They had a long wait at the bus terminal. Abuelita purchased the tickets while Gaby sat in the waiting area eating snacks Abuelita had generously bought for her. Gaby was amazed by her. It seemed she was not afraid of asking anyone for anything. She approached the ticket booth, demanding tickets to Monterrey, requesting departure times, and even negotiating the price. Because of Gaby's love for her abuelita and the force of her personality, Abuelita Fela became another of Gaby's heroes. As Gaby got older, Abuelita seemed to only grow stronger in character and more deserving of respect.

During the three-hour bus ride to Monterrey, Gaby had plenty of time to discuss future trips with Abuelita. She promised to take Gaby with her on all her summer trips. When they arrived at the bus terminal in Monterrey for the first time, it is safe to say that Abuelita was a bit lost. The bus terminal was too busy; people were running left and right, and outside there was an endless line of taxi cabs. There was no one to call and inform that they had arrived. The terminal had no phone. When Gaby realized Abuelita was lost, she was suddenly afraid and started crying. Abuelita got upset and held Gaby's arm, saying, "There is no reason for you to cry." We will find a way to get to your aunt's house."

Gaby wasn't completely sure that Abuelita was not lying to her, but she wiped her tears with her dress and held Abuelita's hand tightly. Abuelita then assured her, "We all speak the same language here, and we can ask these people. Haven't you ever heard the saying, '*Preguntando se llega a Roma?* (Asking all the way to Rome)' That's exactly what we are going to do. We will ask around until we find someone who knows the way to your aunt's house."

In the end Abuelita came up with a better plan. She stopped a taxi and gave the driver a piece of paper with the address of the aunt's house scribbled on it. After a while, the cab dropped them off a few streets away from her aunt's front door. Gaby was very relieved to see her aunt sitting in the yard outside of her house. Abuelita then said, 'Gaby, we got here and we are safe. There was no need for you to be afraid; you are with me. And after this, there is no reason for you to be afraid, even without me.'

"Abuelita Fela's impact on Gaby's life continues to be huge. Gaby still loves and respects her abuelita's compassion, courage, and strength. She was not afraid of anything and she was always in control of herself. Every summer after that trip, until the summer of 1989, Gaby traveled with her. Every year Gaby's admiration for her grew. Even as Abuelita was growing older and weaker, she remained undaunted and determined to overcome all obstacles.

After their last trip to Abasolo, Tamaulipas, in August of 1989, Abuelita Fela stayed at Gaby's home for a few days. Gaby did not understand then, but that stay was a way for them to begin to say good-bye. Abuelita seemed to know her time was near. Gaby and Abuelita still slept together, but Sanjuanita kept Gaby busy doing chores so she would spend less time with Abuelita. The last night Abuelita slept with her, Gaby had a nightmare. In this frightening dream, for some unexplained reason, the Garza's home fell apart, brick by brick, until there was nothing but a thick cloud of dust filling the air. Gaby was terrified as she stood in the middle of the pile of bricks, and there was no one to help her, no parents and no Abuelita. Gaby woke up screaming. Abuelita took her in her arms and, although Gaby was nearly as big as Abuelita, Abuelita cradled her like a baby, telling her that everything was okay. Gaby tried explaining her nightmare to her, but she didn't allow it.

At seven thirty in the morning the next day, Abuelita was already getting ready to catch the eight o'clock train to go back home. They ate breakfast in a rush before Sanjuanita and Gaby walked her to the train station. Gaby was to see her again in a few weeks, possibly to start another trip. She knew Abuelita was going to come over often, because Sanjuanita was close to eight months pregnant with another brother, German.

When Sanjuanita and Gaby got back to the house, Gaby immediately went to her room to cry. Before she had a chance for any tears, she saw Abuelita's pillow and a sweater on Gaby's bed. Those left items put her emotional outburst on hold. Gaby thought at the time Abuelita had forgotten and had left them accidentally. She was happy to have something that belonged to Abuelita; the pillow held Abuelita's scent. Gaby told her mom about the sweater and pillow. She tearfully asked if she could keep the pillow until Abuelita's next visit. Gaby promised she would not keep them but give them back when she next saw her Abuelita Fela. September came and went and Gaby didn't see Abuelita. During September, Abuelita's only sister visited, and Sanjuanita mentioned that Gaby and Abuelita had traveled together. Gaby was already in school, and her parents were so busy taking care of harvesting the crops that they could not afford time to take her over to Abuelita's house. Gaby finally got to see her on October 9, when Sanjuanita gave birth to her brother, German. Abuelita was in Monterrey when Sanjuanita's labor pains began. As soon as she was told of the birth, she took a bus to Rio Bravo then went directly to the hospital. The new baby was perfect and beautiful and the topic of all conversations. Although she tried, Gaby did not have a chance to tell her about the pillow and sweater. The next time Gaby saw her, she was lying on her bed in her house, pale, cold, and stiff. She could take Gaby on no more trips and there would be no more of the game of hiding from Sanjuanita while eating forbidden foods. On November 22, 1989, Abuelita Fela passed away of a massive heart attack.

Gaby remembers they were driving back from her dad's ranch when her mom got the news. A relative stopped her and said, 'Your mom is very ill; you need to immediately go to her house.' What was normally a thirty-minute drive to Abuelita's took Sanjuanita about fifteen minutes.

Sanjuanita was not crying, so Gaby had no clue what was going on except that they were in a hurry, and that Sanjuanita seemed very concerned. They went inside Abuelita's house and there she was, looking sound asleep in her room with a coffin laid out next to her. Gaby knew she was dead because that is what she was told, but she was too young and without experience to understand what that meant. She couldn't understand why people were crying, or why Sanjuanita kept asking the same question over and over, 'Why, God? Why?'

It took a long time for Gaby to realize that she would never travel with Abuelita again. All she had left were memories of a strong, courageous, and determined woman, the good teachings she gave her, and the pillow and sweater she left behind on Gaby's bed. Gaby knows now that the memories, the pillow, and the sweater were all Abuelita had to leave her, and along with the memories, it was enough.

Gaby sees Abuelita in her mother sometimes. She sees a little of Abuelita in herself sometimes. Gaby likes to think about and remember all the good things Abuelita taught her. She still enjoys the feel and smell of her pillow, even after so many years. One time Abuelita told Gaby that she would become a shining star up in the sky after she died, and if Gaby looked for her, she would always find her. After Abuelita's funeral, Gaby picked a star, the brightest star, and named it Fela. Gaby can locate the star no matter the time of the year. She knows it is Abuelita's star, and she knows Abuelita would have wanted to be the star she picked. Sometimes, Gaby thinks she sees it wink at her, and she sheds a few tears in memory of their good times together and her sadness that Abuelita is gone.

GROWING UP WITH ABUELO PABLO

When she was a little girl, Gaby's paternal grandfather, *Abuelo* (Grandfather) Pablo, lived in a mud and grass house set in a grove of trees beside a large field on *El Rancho Las Maravillas*. When she was very young, Gaby loved being at his house of mud and sticks and would visit him as often as she was allowed. Despite the contrast in their ages and outlooks, Gaby and her Abuelo Pablo had a great working relationship. She acted the part of the *chiflada* (spoiled little girl) and in his peculiar way, Abuelo Pablo encouraged it while playing the part of an intolerant curmudgeon.

Abuelo Pablo bought *pan dulce* (sweet bread) every Saturday to eat for breakfast over the next week. He bought seven pieces of pan, one pan dulce for each day. To keep rodents out of his breakfast, he stored it all in a tin suspended by a wire from the ceiling, higher than Gaby could reach without help. Gaby knew he kept pan dulces, and where he kept them. On her visits, she would ask Abuelo Pablo for one of the sweet treats, but he would always deny her permission and threaten to hide them. On one visit, she asked as always and he denied her permission even more emphatically than usual. However, later that day Gaby found a chair standing under the tin. If she stood on the chair, Gaby could reach it for herself, and she knew no one but Abuelo Pablo could have placed the chair just so. Abuelo Pablo caught her stealing his pan dulce and scolded her horribly, but since she had already taken a bite, he let her eat it "instead of wasting it." On each of her visits after that, he would deny her permission to eat a pan dulce, but the chair would always be set in place for her to help herself. Sometimes he would catch her and sometimes she got away free. Either way it was exciting and fun for her, and she believes it was fun for him also. It was a way for him to share with his grandchild without giving up his image as a cranky old man.

A shovel was the only tool Abuelo Pablo Used to dig a garden behind his house each spring. He seeded it with watermelons and vegetables and tended it lovingly. He spent part of each day caring for the plants and gathering produce. In addition, he raised chickens and ducks. Gaby loved the ducks, and she especially loved having them swarm around her. She tried many ways to catch and attract them, but the only way she ever successfully coaxed them to come around her was to feed them. But Abuelo Pablo forbade her from feeding the ducks. However, she knew where the feed was kept, and sometimes when Abuelo Pablo would go inside the house or out to his garden, she would sneak some feed from the sack and spread it all around her. Soon she would be surrounded by ducks, and soon after that she would be harshly scolded by Abuelo Pablo. But what could he do? Throwing his hands up he would exclaim in mock disgust, "I cannot pick up all the small grains of feed faster than the ducks!" Then with an air of resignation, he would say, "What is done is done." He would continue scolding her under his breath as he walked away, waving his hands in the air and mumbling.

When Gaby was with Abuelo Pablo and the watermelons were ripe, he would occasionally cut one for him and Gaby to eat together. Grandfather and granddaughter would share a feast of sweet, juicy, freshly-cut watermelon.

Though he had no teeth, Abuelo Pablo could eat watermelon. Gaby would watch him with great curiosity and wonder, accompanied by more than a little giggling. Using just his gums, he mashed the juice from the meat and swallowed, then spit out the seeds quickly before taking another bite. He could eat watermelon faster using his gums than Gaby could with a full set of teeth. She marveled also at the speed with which Abuelo Pablo could eat his favorite Brach's orange slices candy. He could eat five slices in less time than it took her to eat one.

In the front and to the west side of Abuelo Pablo's house, there was a water well that Gaby loved to throw rocks into so she could hear the splash and watch the ripples on the darkened surface of the water far below. She loved hearing the splash and its echoes, even when she could not see the ripples. Not being able to see the splash increased the wonder and mystery of the experience. There was an element of surprise about the noise of an unseen splash that Gaby enjoyed. Her giggling and laughing usually brought her grandfather outside, angry about yet another trespass. When Abuelo Pablo would catch her throwing rocks into his well, he would banish her to the other side of the house. In order to avoid the appearance of guilt, Gaby would sometimes stand with her back to the well, pretending to do something else while actually throwing rocks over her shoulder toward the well. Occasionally a rock would hit the mark, splashing into the dark well, and she would be delighted by the mysterious splash. But when Abuelo Pablo would amble over to see what she was doing, she would pretend to be busy away from the well, and Abuelo Pablo would pretend he did not know what she was doing. Abuelo Pablo's fussing, quarreling, and feigned outrage were simply too much fun to pass up.

Whenever Gaby had gotten herself into too much trouble, and Abuelo Pablo had had enough, he would scold her and call her names to emphasize his displeasure. Gaby enjoyed making him upset enough to hear this scolding. It was always the same. He would call her *Guerca Fea! Prieta! Peluda! Dientona!*

Guerca is a term Abuelo Pablo used that is not really a word; it is a slang term for girl, but not just any girl, it is an insult indicating low class. *Fea* means ugly. *Prieta* means dark-skinned. Abuelo Pablo and his family were light-skinned with matching light eyes. It is common for light-skinned Mexicans to look down on dark-skinned Mexicans, assuming them to be of a lower class. *Peluda* means hairy (Gaby always wore her dark hair long.)

Dientona means big-toothed. So roughly translated, he would call her an ugly, hairy, dark-skinned, big-toothed, low-class girl. She never took the insults seriously, because she knew that he didn't mean any of it. The light of fun shining in his eyes could not be hidden. He spoiled her, but always pretended that she was the cause of too much trouble.

During Easter celebrations, Abuelo Pablo's mud-and-stick house on El Rancho Las Maravillas was the main gathering place for all his family, neighbors, and a few invited visitors. For Gaby, visitors meant children to play with at the fiesta. Gaby would tell the other children all the tricks she had learned at her grandfather's house and act out how upset he would get, but the other children were not allowed the privilege of this fun. When other children were around, Abuelo Pablo would remove the chair from under the sweet bread, hide the duck feed, and cover the well when he was not drawing water. When only Gaby was around, all the safeguards were removed, and they played their wonderful and exciting game of cat and mouse. Gaby always looked forward to her visits to Abuelo Pablo's house of mud and sticks.

GROWING UP WITH MAMA

As a young girl growing up in rural, hot and dusty Tamaulipas, Mexico, one of Gaby's greatest pleasures was fulfilling her natural desire to learn. Her most devoted teacher was her loving mother. Long before she was of an age to go to school, Gaby's mother began instilling in her a love of learning and achievement in academics. Her mother taught her from very young to dream of her future. She taught Gaby letters and sounds and basic mathematics. From the beginning of this instruction, Gaby was a quick and able student. She loved to learn and was eager to please her mother. She loved the lessons, but even more, Gaby loved the focused attention and nurturing she received from her mother. These were warm and happy times with Sanjuanita. Gaby looked forward with increasing anticipation to the day she could go to kindergarten and learn in a real school from a real teacher.

Sanjuanita tried to fill Gaby's time with the learning that she herself had been denied as a child. Having received little formal education herself, Sanjuanita respected education and was determined that her daughter would have opportunities she had never received to learn from and about the world she would live in. She remembered the feeling of being ignorant while those she was among were well informed. She remembered the embarrassment and the desire to run away from being the butt of jokes because of the things she was never taught. She worked hard to assure that her daughter would not experience those feelings, but would instead feel empowered by knowledge. Sanjuanita had seen the change in her mother, Fela, after her father died. She liked the confidence and the assurance her mother seemed to gain and wanted that confidence and independence for her daughter. Consequently, part of Gaby's education came from the intentionally frequent and close contact she had with Abuelita Fela.

Of course, there are things that mothers and fathers teach their children that come from no book or any particular purpose, but from who they are. Men who are honest in all their dealings don't have to say much to their children about honesty. The honest man's children understand that honesty is important because they see it in their father. The same goes with all learned character traits for which there is little in the way of curriculum. Sanjuanita taught much to her children simply by being herself. She taught kindness, gentleness, and perseverance in the face of cruelty'. She taught a dependence on God when there seems little hope. She taught her children to make the best of life's twists and turns, realizing that all situations are temporary be they good or ill. She taught her children the value of family and caring for those in need. Sanjuanita taught what it means to be a good citizen of the world; she taught faith, hope, and charity.

Sanjuanita taught her children the greatest lesson anyone can hope to learn in their walk with others. She taught them through example again and again in her daily dealings with them, their father, and those not even related to the family. She taught her children the virtue of a forgiving spirit. She taught these lessons well enough that Gaby formed a wonderfully strong character during her youth.

5

The Malady

Once when Gaby was still very young, she went with her mother to El Rancho Las Maravillas to milk the cows. Actually, Gaby's plan was to play with the calves. She loved that they would flee just out of arms' reach from her when she ran at them. It was about nine in the morning, still cool, but the day was warming. While Sanjuanita took care of the milking, Gaby chased the calves around the milking area. The calves were dependent on their mother's milk and always hungry, so they refused to stray far from the cows. They ran from the little girl in circles around and around the milking area instead of off into the pasture or field. They were waiting for their mothers to be released to have their chance at milk. Gaby squealed with laughter as she watched them run, chasing them in a circle with her mother and the cows in the center, always in sight. After Gaby had run a few laps around the water well and back, Sanjuanita continued to see the calves running in the circle, but Gaby was nowhere to be seen.

The grass was tall in the milking area, making it easy for a small child to hide. Thinking Gaby might be playing a trick on her, she called out, but she received no answer. Growing fearful that something serious had happened, she left the pail half full of milk and hurried to find her child. Sure enough, Gaby was lying on the grass and not moving; she had fainted. Her mother quickly revived her and cooled her down. She seemed fine, no worse from the experience. After that first time chasing calves, fainting became a kind of habit with Gaby. She fainted at church, at school, in the yard, or wherever she happened to be when she got too hot.

6

Vanessa

When she was four, Gaby's mother decided she should learn to care for a pet. Gaby asked for a cat. Her Abuelo Pablo, who still lived on El Rancho Las Maravillas in his house of mud and sticks, had lots of kittens that Gaby loved to play with. He allowed her to pick any kitten she wanted. She loved them all and thought they were all beautiful but could have only one. Finally, she picked a white Siamese mix with beautiful blue eyes; Abuelo Pablo gave it to her. Gaby thought the kitten had a very elegant walk, and it reminded her of the beautiful lady in an elegant white dress who walked through clouds at the beginning of one of her mother's *novelas* (soap operas). She named the kitten Vanessa, after the actress in the white dress. Gaby told everyone that the cat was so elegant she could walk across the room without even touching the floor.

For a while, Vanessa was the center of Gaby's universe. Everywhere Gaby went, she took Vanessa. She enjoyed playing with the cat, talking to her and feeding her. When Gaby would lie down to take a nap, Vanessa often served as a willing pillow, lying still, purring, and pawing the air in pleasure. But the pleasure Gaby found in Vanessa was short-lived. After a few months, Vanessa disappeared and was never found. Gaby was saddened by the loss of her companion and never discovered what had happened to her beloved Vanessa. Papi said that she was not responsible enough to have any more pets as she had lost Vanessa. Papi never gave Gaby permission to get another pet.

7

School in Mexico

KINDERGARTEN

The school that served all the children of the ejido consisted of two buildings, one for kindergarten and one for first through sixth grade. After months of anticipation, the day finally arrived for Gaby's first day of kindergarten to begin in the building adjacent to Escuela Salome' Gomez. Gaby was ready to attend kindergarten; she had more academic knowledge than most of her peers, and she was anxious to begin. On that long awaited first day of school, she got up early, dressed in a hurry, ate breakfast, and left the house, chattering excitedly and ready to walk the short distance down the street to the kindergarten building. But before Gaby could get out of the driveway, Sanjuanita dropped a bombshell.

KINDERGARTEN FOR EJIDO BUENA VISTA

Sometime during 1982, before Gaby was old enough to go to school, the head professor of the elementary school announced to the residents of Buena Vista that the reason their children could not participate in local academic competitions (similar to UIL in the US) was because the kids were learning in first grade what they should have learned in kindergarten. He explained that the majority of the Buena Vista children at every grade level were about a year behind other school children in Mexico, especially in reading and mathematics. He told them that if residents wanted their children to be involved in extracurricular activities, such as yearly math competitions, parents needed to help by teaching their children the basics of school at home or build a kindergarten and find a teacher. After this announcement, the residents realized that they were not prepared to teach their five-year-olds what was necessary. Instead the people of Ejido Buena Vista gathered together to provide their children a kindergarten. They pitched in the necessary money to buy a small-frame house that had been empty for some time, move it to the vacant lot, and to make it into a kindergarten. Overcoming great financial difficulties, they also recruited a teacher. Fortunately, a recent graduate from the *secundaria* (high school) accepted the job offer and took on the role of kindergarten teacher for the first year.

During the summer, four-year-old Gaby watched the parents of the ejido working together to clean the lot the small house stood on, and paint the building. They installed a playground of worn out tractor tires and swings for the children to play on during recess. The new kindergarten was taking shape. The ejido parents painted the outer walls of the classroom sky blue. They were excited about the new school emerging from their hard work, and they were proud of their accomplishment. The closer the kindergarten came to being completed, the more Gaby's excitement built. The first day the kindergarten opened in Ejido Buena Vista, Gaby and her mom walked her older brother past the blue building to the elementary school; young Gilberto, Beto Jr., was already attending fourth grade. As they passed by, Gaby saw kids being walked to the door of the kindergarten classroom by their parents. She was very jealous of those children—they were very lucky to be in school. She wanted to be one of those kids, to have a teacher and to learn. She was dying to be one of those kids wearing a cute uniform. Her mother assured Gaby she would be attending school the next year.

The kindergarten building and playground were separated from the rest of the elementary school by a hog-wire fence. The kindergarten was set up in a lot next to the existing school grounds. The ejido residents were very proud they had a kindergarten that they had built and staffed themselves.

From the time her mother first told her about school, a fire of longing was ignited deep in Gaby's heart, a longing to go to school and learn. During the first year the kindergarten was open, Gaby would leave her house at different times of the day, walk to the kindergarten, and hang on to the fence to watch the kindergarten activities. She was anticipating and longing for her own first day in kindergarten. She loved seeing the children running and playing and the teacher coming outside to get them. Gaby watched them line up outside the kindergarten room, then march in together with their hands behind their backs, often reciting the alphabet or counting. Later she would listen to the children as they recited their phonic sounds. She would also listen carefully as they rehearsed their numbers, reciting them silently to herself. Each time she watched and listened, she imagined herself among the children and enjoyed a vicarious feeling of accomplishment. It did not occur or matter to her that she already knew most of what was being taught, and she was learning well the few things she did not already know. Gaby would return home and excitedly tell her mother what she had seen and what she had learned each day while listening. Sanjuanita made mental notes of all Gaby learned and began making a decision concerning Gaby's schooling.

BEGINNING SCHOOL

Sanjuanita Garza was proactive when it came to her children's studies. At the end of each school year, she would request unfinished or leftover workbooks for her children to complete during the summer. She also asked for advice from the *maestro* (teacher) at the school in developing her summer curricula for her children. At the beginning of the summer of 1983, when Gaby was four, Sanjuanita requested a first-grade workbook for Gaby. The workbook was one of Sanjuanita's many efforts to enrich her daughter's life in the direction of learning academics.

Gaby's academic learning had begun before she was two. Her brother had been in an accident with Papi Beto and spent months in a cast that ran from his hips to his ankles. During this time, he could not play outside.

Sanjuanita kept him busy by teaching him. The television was practically never turned on at the Garza home, and certainly never when Sanjuanita was teaching. The time was used instead for schooling. Young Gilberto quickly learned his ABC's, numbers, colors, and shapes. He developed a hunger for learning and moved quickly through the material. He requested more challenging work. Sanjuanita had no choice but to teach him the math and history that she knew. Gaby learned along with him, at a slower pace because she was more than three years younger, but she learned a considerable amount of the material and retained well what she learned.

These exercises continued over the next two years, even when Gilberto, Jr. attended school and she stayed home. As soon as he arrived home in the afternoon, she would sit with him during homework time and pretend to have homework of her own; she would complete her brother's assignments the best she could.

When Sanjuanita noticed Gaby was getting bored with the work, she asked the professor for a more difficult workbook. She completed the book over the summer. It was a first-grade workbook, and she completed it two summers before she was to begin first grade.

The first day of the school year, when Gaby was four and still too young to attend school, Sanjuanita escorted Gilberto, Jr. to school and mentioned Gaby's accomplishments to the professor. He said, "She is a bright girl. If she is ready, she can start first grade next year and skip kindergarten." Gaby was upset by this, but the conversation did not stick in her mind. She hung on to the dream that she would begin her schooling in kindergarten the next fall; she would wear the uniform, recite the ABC's, count to twenty, and play on the embedded tires. However, this dream was not realized on her first day of school.

NO KINDERGARTEN FOR GABY

Gaby was not to go to kindergarten; she was to go to first grade. Sanjuanita thought Gaby would be pleased, but she was not. Twenty-plus years later, Gaby understands her mother's decision, but she still has emotional regrets about not being allowed to attend kindergarten with her peers. Her dreams of attending kindergarten were ruined by the care and attention her mother had given to her learning at home. She already knew more than they would teach in kindergarten. On that first morning of school when Gaby was five, Gaby's mother told her to go directly to the first-grade room. In that moment, Gaby recalled the discussion that had occurred between the teacher and Mrs. Garza that fateful day the previous year. The decision to move Gaby along to the first grade was made without her input. She wanted desperately to attend kindergarten. She cried, stomped her feet, crossed her arms, and pouted, all to no avail. Her mother stuck to the plan she and the teacher had agreed upon. Gaby was to begin first grade while the other five-year-olds began kindergarten.

Long before that first day of school when Gaby was five, Sanjuanita had promised that when she turned five, Gaby would go to kindergarten and experience all that she had imagined with such delicious anticipation. She begged her mother and cried, but Sanjuanita knew that her child could learn nothing more by attending kindergarten and would soon tire of school because she would be learning nothing new. Gaby had to go on to first grade. It was decided. Finally Gaby relented, stopped her begging and crying, uncrossed her arms, and walked dejectedly with her mother to her first day of school in the first grade. She had a lump in her throat and felt empty. Sanjuanita had an equally large lump in her throat. She had not intended to fool her daughter and had not been aware of the extreme emotional attachment Gaby had built up to the idea of attending kindergarten.

When faced with disappointment, most people will blame man or God, cry, throw a fit, generally be miserable, and then perhaps look for a way to retaliate against those they feel have wronged them. However, a select few will turn their attention to finding a way to make the best of the new situation life has presented to them. On the way to her first day of first grade, while kicking up dust in the middle of the dirt road, a realization began to grow in Gaby; the professor had high expectations of her! He believed in her! She could not express the idea, but she knew it deep down, and it began to work on her mind. The professor wanted to teach her first grade and thought she could do it. For a few steps this scared her, and she almost turned around and attempted to drag her mother back home, but in a few more steps something inside her started growing again. The fire for learning new things began again burning inside her heart. That fire coupled with the confidence expressed by the revered Profesor Vargas gave her a different feeling. In those few steps, she determined that she was not going to fail the professor or her mother. If the professor had confidence in her, she would not let him down. She wanted to be an outstanding student, not just an okay one. She would strive to be the best student the professor ever had. She was sad that she was not allowed to attend kindergarten, but by the time she walked into the first-grade classroom on her very first day of school, she had a new resolve; she was a committed student. Thus began her efforts to learn and impress her teacher in school, efforts that would continue unabated for the next six years.

SEÑOR JOSE VARGAS

The feeling of sadness Gaby felt on the way to first grade continued to morph into the desire to achieve, especially as she got to know Señor Jose Jaime Vargas, her teacher. Señor Vargas traveled by bus to Ejido Buena Vista from Reynosa, Tamaulipas, Mexico. He made the trip on the bus then walked a little over a mile to Escuela Salome' Gomez, then returned home each day of the school year. Señor Vargas was a dedicated educator who gave a significant part of his life to the children and families of Ejido Buena Vista. The word "gave" is used appropriately, because Señor Vargas could have demanded to be transferred to a school closer to his home many years before Gaby entered school. In a larger school, he could have made more money and stayed closer to home, turning the long daily commute over to a younger and less experienced teacher. Instead, he continued to take the lower pay and make the long trip to serve the small isolated community and its children. Gaby sensed the quiet courage and dedication in this wonderful man and soon had a hero from whom she was eager to win respect.

SCHOOL

There was little money in the ejido to support the community school after paying Señor Vargas' meager salary. There were few supplies such as pencils and paper, no desks, few books, no heat during the cold couple of months and no air-conditioning for the hot season from early spring to late fall. Chalk was in short supply, and there was never an adequate chalkboard. Fruit crates became desks when they were stood on end and benches when they were turned facedown. Both sides of a piece of paper were used, and many of the graded exams in school were oral to avoid using the school's meager supply. The smoothest wall often became a chalkboard for an activity then was carefully wiped down for another lesson.

The school building consisted of two rooms each approximately fifteen feet square, side by side, lined up north to south, each with a single outside door opening to the east. There were windows along the entire west wall of the building, none of which had glass. Those windows were great for ventilation, but they placed the temperature and lighting of each room at the mercy of North Mexican weather. The rooms were only truly comfortable very few days of the year. They were too hot and too bright in the early fall and late spring, and too cold and too dark during most of the winter. They were well-lit during sunny weather, poorly-lit during cloudy days, arid in dry weather, and damp when it rained. Whatever the weather was outside, was the weather inside the classrooms.

Each classroom held three grades, each grade facing a different direction: north, east, and south. The first room usually held first, third, and fifth grade. The second room held second, fourth, and sixth grade. The professor would take turns teaching the different levels of material. Once lecture was over for one grade, a written exercise was assigned, which allowed the professor time to move on to the next grade's lecture. He would also have to run from room to room checking on the kids' progress and handing out additional assignments. At times the professor would take on an aspiring teacher to do his or her observation hours at Escuela Salome' Gomez. In Mexico, each prospective teacher had to volunteer in a working school for a period of time and receive a recommendation from the teacher of record before they could be certified to teach a class of their own. This extra person would help Professor Vargas tremendously, though for only a few weeks. While he taught the kids in one room, the fledgling teacher would stay in the other room watching over the kids. Some of these volunteers would stay on as a student-teacher at the ejido for a few weeks, maybe even months, but because of the long commute, they would never return the following year. Keeping teachers in the ejido was always a struggle. If it were not for the dedication of Profesor Vargas, Ejido Buena Vista would probably not have had a teacher for many months out of the year, and perhaps not at all.

The school's setup, having three grades in each room, helped Gaby develop her skills. She was a fast learner, and loved to get her work done ahead of time. Gaby stayed busy and never got bored in school. She completed most assignments before anyone else, which allowed her time to pay attention to the lectures being given to the other groups and even attempt a few of the older students' assignments. She didn't comprehend everything being taught to the older children, but some things made sense to her and she was able to memorize things she did not understand. She was even able to learn from the lectures given younger students. Those lectures filled in any gaps in her learning and served as a great review of concepts she had already learned.

Profesor Vargas paid close attention to those of his students who seemed particularly dedicated. He soon noticed the consistent effort and dedication of Gaby Garza. She received many positive comments on her papers and reports home from Profesor Vargas as she progressed through the year. She enjoyed receiving these comments and proudly displayed them to her mother and anyone else who would look or listen. Her mother showed great appreciation for her daughter's dedication and Profesor Vargas' encouragement.

During the summer before Gaby entered fourth grade, the community made some improvements. They added a third classroom and a small office for the professor. The addition was built by the people of the town, and it helped the professor by allowing him to have only two grades in each room and a place to store teaching materials.

PARENTAL INVOLVEMENT IN LA ESCUELA SALOME' GOMEZ

Parents in the ejido played very important roles in the school system, making the education of their children a community effort and concern. During cold weather, open fires were built inside the rooms and tended by parents in order to provide some measure of comfort to the children as they learned to read, write, and perform arithmetic. Since most of the parents were farmers, during very cold or wet weather, the men of Ejido Buena Vista had time to take their turns tending the flames. There was no food program for the school, so the women either got together to feed the children en masse, or each brought their own children lunches to ensure they received the occasional hot meal. Usually a lunch of cold tacos was packed in newspaper at home and brought to school by the children.

Frequently, a learning project in the school would culminate in a demonstration, presentation, or play. The entire village would be invited to gather and see the children's work. Parents would provide food for the meeting, materials for costumes, skills for building the necessary stage or sets, or sewing costumes. After all that involvement in preparing for the school program, parents and other members of the ejido became an audience for the displays, musicals, and plays. Project demonstration nights were festive events for the people of the ejido. Generally, after the children had made their presentations, everyone ate at their version of a pot luck, and occasionally the men who played a musical instrument would entertain while everyone else danced.

Parents were very involved in making sure homework was done well and children behaved themselves properly in school. Neither slacking nor misbehaving was tolerated by Señor Vargas. He quickly called in parents when he needed their help with a child. The parents just as quickly provided the needed motivation and discipline for their own children. Neither inattention nor the breaking of rules were tolerated by parents or Profesor Vargas, and disrespect was not an issue.

Gaby attended the village school from first through sixth grade. Profesor Vargas was her teacher each of the six years. Despite being a year younger than her classmates, she quickly won a place at the head of her class. From the beginning of first grade, Gaby was driven by a desire to earn Señor Vargas' signature.

Each year one student from each grade was chosen by Profesor Vargas as the top student for that year. Shortly after the first day of school, Gaby was shown an award earned by a student the previous year. Señor Vargas' bold signature stood at the bottom of the certificate and the student's name was just as boldly printed in the top center. That intricate signature with a flourish drawn underneath immediately became her goal for the year. She wanted that signature at the bottom of an award with her name printed on it. For that signature she was willing to work harder, learn more, and focus more than anyone else. If she saw someone working hard, she worked even harder, doing everything to the best of her abilities and more. Gaby earned that signature each year from first to fourth grade.

The year Gaby was in fifth grade, Claudia Patricia Davalos Alvarado attended La Escuela Salome' Gomez, also in the fifth grade. Claudia proved to be a good friend, but also the greatest competition Gaby had for the coveted signature. Most days after school, Claudia walked home with Gaby to play after the hard day at school. Often during that year, Claudia received higher grades than Gaby on assignments. Whenever this occurred, Gaby would call a halt to playtime in order to study so she could do better than Claudia on the next assignment. On more than one occasion, Gaby sent Claudia home early from playing after school so she could spend the rest of her afternoon studying. She worried that Claudia might be the one to receive Profesor Vargas' signature that year. She dedicated herself even more to her schoolwork. She wanted that signature!

At the end of her fifth-grade year, Gaby again earned her certificate with the signature with the flourish and her name printed in the center. Out of the six years she attended the school, Gaby earned that signature six times. Profesor Vargas never called on her parents for their assistance in correcting or motivating Gaby. Their help was never required.

8

Moving to Los Estados Unidos

FROM MEXICO TO MERCEDEZ

German, Gaby's little brother, was born in 1989. Toward the end of the summer of 1990, with her family complete, Sanjuanita Garza determined that it was time to cross into the US to visit some of her family living in Texas. She wanted to make the visit before the children began school and before harvest time. She took her children to the border crossing at Nuevo Progresso, a small Mexican town across the border from Progresso, Texas, in the United States. After asking questions about the process, she found she would have to apply for a visitor's card. Having that card would allow her to travel in Texas along the border for a short period of time. When that time was up, she would have to return to Mexico. She applied because, even with the time constraints, she figured she could still manage to make her visits and be back in Mexico without violating any rules.

When she returned her completed application to the officials, she was told by one of the American border guards that she must have her husband with her to get her visitor's card. Sanjuanita thought the demand was strange, but figured that it must only be a part of the identification process. She did not question the request and used the border station's phone to call for Beto to come help her. Beto immediately started for Progresso.

When Beto arrived, the conversation with the border agents changed to a different subject. Ms. Escamilla, the border guard who had demanded his presence, asked him for his identification card then began asking questions about things unfamiliar to the family. Neither Sanjuanita nor her children totally understood the questions asked or the answers Beto gave. There were two problems with the conversation. First, the guard mostly spoke in English, and the family knew little of the language. Second, Beto's answers in Spanish did not make sense to them. The conversation seemed to be about another family. Finally, Officer Escamilla stopped talking and went to another room. When she came back, she spoke to Beto in Spanish, "Sir, we have to take you in. You are breaking the law." She switched into English, saying, "You cannot have two residences."

Gaby had learned enough English that she understood some of the words, but not their implications. She thought maybe the guard meant two citizenships. Officer Escamilla took Beto's US resident card and gave him a choice. "You can go to the US, and get a Permanent Resident Card within a year, or you can go back to Mexico. But if you go to Mexico, you can never come back to the US"

Unknown to Sanjuanita and her children, Mr. Garza had another family, a wife and children, who lived in Weslaco, Texas. Mr. Garza immediately made the decision to move to the United States without talking it over with the family. Even to the rest of the family, who still knew nothing of Beto's other family, moving to the US seemed the easiest thing to do. Though puzzled by the statement about two residences, neither Sanjuanita nor the children grasped the significance.

Beto Garza was already renting a house on a lot a short distance outside of Mercedez, Texas, less than ten miles from his other family. No one in Sanjuanita's immediate family knew of the house. Mr. Garza secretly weighed his options; if he decided to stay in Mexico, he would not be able to earn the money necessary to support two families. His earning potential was better in the United States.

Once the decision was made to move to Texas, the family returned to their home in Buena Vista and, somewhat in shock at the turn of events, gathered their clothes and what necessities they could carry across the border. The oldest son, Gilberto, was fifteen and capable of running the family farm. He took over the care of the Garzas' holdings in Mexico. Since he was named after his father, he could sign Mr. Garza's papers without lying, and no one would know that the management had changed hands.

Beto also owned a piece of property on the Texas side of the border with a small house. He had never revealed to his family that he owned it let alone how he had obtained it. Regardless, when they moved to the US, the property was being rented by another family and was not available for them to use. The property had a small wooden house on it painted blue and only had two rooms: a kitchen/living room and a sleeping room so was really too small for the couple and four children.

When they came across the border, one of Beto's brothers heard of their situation and offered to let the family stay with him until they could find a decent place to live. Beto took the offer without consulting Sanjuanita. It was a disappointing surprise to the rest of the Garza family when they were told they were going to live with unfamiliar cousins with whom they had little in common and with whom their only contacts had been negative.

Sanjuanita simply obeyed Beto and asked Gaby and her brothers to behave and follow their dad's orders. Gaby didn't like the idea at all. These particular cousins often laughed at her family when they attended family reunions or gatherings. They made fun of the "poor ways" of their Mexican relatives. They jeered at their food, clothing, and lack in the luxuries which are taken for granted in the US. Gaby remembered even the aunts and uncles calling Sanjuanita names. Sanjuanita simply took the insults with her usual grace, but the name-calling would anger Gaby. She wondered, *Why would Papi choose to put his family through such unhappiness!?*

LIFE WITH PRIMOS

Their arrival at their *primos'* (cousins') home burned itself into the memories of the Garza family. The experience was going to be very humbling, and they knew it; everyone in the family knew it, except seemingly Beto. The house was very nice compared to any they had lived in. It was a brick house with three bedrooms, nice shiny floors, drapes, a large kitchen, and a spacious living room. In size it was much like the home in Mexico they had left. Of course all of the furniture and fixtures looked way better than those they had left behind in Mexico, but Gaby still preferred their old house. The cousins' home had air-conditioning, with which Gaby's family was not accustomed. Also there wasn't an outhouse but an inside toilet instead, only one for the entire household.

The older cousins immediately began making insulting comments, veiled comments that were none the less intended to be insults. They made fun of their poor relatives from Mexico, saying things like, "Now you are going to live the good life. You will no longer have to live at your poor ranch." The cousins didn't seem to understand that the "poor ranch" was everything to Gaby and her family. They had been happy at the ranch. The ranch had provided for their needs, and they were very much satisfied with what they had. Best of all, there was no debt; they owned everything they had. Why would the cousins think that living in the United States was better than living at the ranch? Their comments hurt everyone in the family at times, but mostly their comments hurt and enraged Gaby. The cousins taunted her about her clothing made from course cloth, her "Mexican" braids, her shoes, her dark skin, and her lack of 'education.'

Soon after arriving at the primos' home, the family was invited into the dining room where they were treated to a warm meal. Gaby thought it was nice of them to serve hot food and extend a gracious welcome. It was all good and fun until Beto's brother and his wife began defining the relationship and setting rules on the table. Beto and Sanjuanita were to sleep in the boys' room with two of the cousins. The room had a full size bed and a set of bunk beds; there was plenty of space, but no privacy. Gaby's two younger brothers would sleep in the bed with her parents or on the floor, wherever the parents saw fit. Gaby was to sleep in the girls' room, with two of her female cousins. Sanjuanita was to help about the house, doing laundry and cooking.

Sleeping in the girls' room was okay with Gaby at first. She thought that spending more time with the cousins would allow them to play and make friends; then they might not be so harsh in their judgments. Gaby also felt, grudgingly, that she must absorb some of the cousins' mistreatment in order to keep the peace. She tried to believe that their stay with this antagonistic family could be a good thing for all of them.

Things did not go as well as Gaby anticipated. The month that the Garza family lived with the cousins was one long, continuous nightmare for Sanjuanita and her children. Gaby's aunt quickly figured out how to take advantage of Sanjuanita's gratitude and soon made her the "mule" of the house, not a maid because maids get paid. Sanjuanita was made to work hard and ordered about so that the aunt could get by doing very little while blaming Sanjuanita for anything that didn't go well or turn out right.

During the first couple of days, Sanjuanita offered to do much of the housework to show her gratitude for the favor of providing them with a place to stay. She agreed to cook, clean the house, and do part of their laundry. Gaby helped her mother by washing dishes and sweeping the floor. Soon the aunt took their gratitude for granted and placed even more conditions on their stay. Sanjuanita was to be in charge of all the cleaning, all the cooking, and all the laundry. The worst part of it all, and the hardest part for Gaby to watch, was that after Sanjuanita finished all the housework to the very best of her ability, the aunt would criticize her in front of others. She complained that the food was not good, the clothes were not clean, or the house was still dirty even after Sanjuanita had worked and cleaned all day. Gaby was not immune to the slander. She would get publically criticized for not washing the dishes correctly.

In Gaby's eyes, the aunt was being cruel because Sanjuanita was very careful and thorough in her work. She also cooked fine meals for them. Gaby soon figured out that her aunt was always most cruel when Beto's brother would come home to a fine meal and a clean house and thank Sanjuanita for her hard work and compliment her on her cooking, cleaning, and ironing skills. He obviously was not accustomed to seeing his house clean, having clean clothes, and eating a hot meal as soon as he came home. Of course, the aunt was unable to appreciate another woman being complimented in her house. The attention and gratitude given to Sanjuanita angered her, and she released her anger continuously on Gaby and her mom.

Gaby's Papi didn't see much of this drama. By the time Beto got home from work, the rest of the family had been fed, and Sanjuanita had dinner ready for him. She served him without complaining. He was gone most of the day, working hard, and witnessed none of the abuse Sanjuanita took all day. Gaby tried to tell him how hard it was to live with her uncle's family and urged him to take them somewhere else; the children even offered to go back to Mexico and live on the ranch without Beto until he could come back to live with them. Gaby tried to explain that it was hard adapting to the ways of another family. She told him they were at the mercy of the relatives, and the relatives were not friendly. She explained further that her mother was not used to cooking in someone else's kitchen; they had ingredients she was not familiar with and pots and pans that didn't cook well. The refrigerator was filled with frozen items and there was not enough fresh produce to make decent meals. In the morning, they had to wait to use the bathroom until the uncle's family was finished. Gaby tried to intercede for her mother, explaining to her father that Sanjuanita was tired of doing their housework, because the relatives, especially the aunt, were never content with the quality of work. Even the cousins, the children, had begun to complain to Sanjuanita and order her about like a servant. Gaby further explained that the family needed more privacy than the arrangement was providing. Beto Garza ignored their pleas and asked his family to "help him" by not complaining. The relatives did help the Garza family in one very important way. They did help Gaby and her brothers register for school.

9

School in the United States

REGISTRATION

Grades one through six at the Escuela Salome' Gomez, under instruction by Professor Vargas, were taught in a total of three rooms and by one teacher. The rooms were unheated in the winter and not cooled during the summer. While in school in Mexico, Gaby ate breakfast at home, and if she had a midday meal, it was because her mother sent it with her in the morning or brought it to her at the school. In Ejido Bueno Vista there was no question about where she would go to school, and her playmates in the village were her classmates in school. In addition, her parents were welcome to visit the school any time they chose. Parents provided meals, heat, materials for school, and support for their children. Nothing Gaby experienced in her time at Escuela Salome' Gomez prepared her for her school experiences during the next few years in Weslaco Independent School District, Texas.

In the lower Rio Grande Valley of Texas, there were cities much larger than Gaby had ever experienced in Mexico, and even the rural areas of Texas were much more densely populated. She had not thought about how this would impact her schooling, and she could not have known, but the Garzas were in for quite a culture shock. In Mexico, the Garza children were never required to register for school; they simply showed up at the school on the first day of class. The school was less than two blocks away from their house. Immunizations against communicable diseases were required in Mexico, but not in the same quantity and kind as in the US.

In Mexico, parents only had to tell the schoolmaster they had immunized their children. In the US, proof from a clinic was required. In their village, everyone knew where everyone else lived, but in the US, everyone had to prove they lived within the school district's attendance zone. The schoolmaster in Mexico knew Mr. and Mrs. Garza personally, but in the Weslaco school district, Mr. and Mrs. Garza had to prove who they were and that their children were really theirs. The Garza family was not prepared with the necessary documentation to register their children for school in Texas. One of Gaby's cousins, who had been raised in Texas, told Mr. Garza where and when to register for school but did not warn them about the proof they would need or the crowds they would encounter.

Mary Hoge Junior High School, located in the middle of the town of Weslaco, had been set up to intake and preregister all children for the district. The Garza children were to attend Weslaco Independent School District, even though they lived closer to the city of Mercedez. The district had a total enrollment of over eleven-thousand students across fifteen campuses in 1990. Because of the heavy population of migrants in the district, approximately twenty-five percent of the district's children were new each year and were required to register and provide all the necessary documentation. A couple of schools served single grade levels: only first grade or sixth grade. A few were primary schools, serving prekindergarten through second grade, and some served primary and elementary students on the same campus. Two junior-high campuses served the seventh and eighth grades, as well as part of the sixth. There was a schedule designating times for the different grade levels to register for school. The Garzas had been told where to go, but did not know to look for a time schedule for when to show up for registration for the different grade levels or schools.

All this organization that was essential to Weslaco was never needed in Escuela Salome' Gomez.

Early in the morning on registration day, the Garza family showed up at the campus they had been told was the proper place to register. They were on campus before the registration was set to begin, so very few people were already there. When Gaby saw the huge buildings built to hold over a thousand students, she got a sick feeling in her stomach. The size of the buildings seemed very strange and scary to Gaby, who was familiar with the small single school building on the small campus in her small village in Mexico. She wondered how she could possibly be able to remember where she was during the school day, and how she could get home from such a place. She began to feel like there was just too much she did not know how to handle. An overwhelming sickness and fear began taking over her body. When she looked at her mother and father for comfort, she realized they were having the same problem dealing with the size of this new place. They looked as uncomfortable and even as scared as she was.

Mr. Garza soon found out that they were at the right place to register. However, since the cousin had neglected to tell them about the differing time schedule for the different grades, they were very early. Unless they left and came back, they were in for a long wait. Everyone was directed to the cafeteria to register or wait for their turn to register.

Gaby had never been in such a large room. There were many tables set up in long lines where families could file their paperwork and conduct the business of registration. Each table had a sign, indicating which patrons could register at that table and at what times. The timing depended on the grade level and the first letter of their last name. There were also signs to indicate what documents were needed to complete that particular part of the registration. Of course, the Garzas arrived too early to register Gaby for seventh grade. At least, she was *expecting* to register for seventh grade.

After a long wait in line to get to the table for students whose last name began with G and were registering for seventh grade, Mr. Garza was told they were in the right place, but not at the right time. The clerk would not answer any questions, but only tell them when they could return. Gaby had to give up her place in line and wait. The family stood along a wall with other people in the same predicament; most were obviously from Mexico. There were also a few children of migrant workers who had come back to

Weslaco early and others from the US who had also shown up at the wrong time.

While they waited along the cafeteria wall, American people, mostly Hispanic but also a few Whites, passed by them. Some looked over the Garzas and the others from Mexico with curiosity and some with obvious judgment and contempt. Gaby watched a lady's face change as her gaze turned toward the line of recent immigrants; it went from one of pleasant friendliness to one of open disgust. It was the face of someone looking at something dirty and foul.

Gaby felt as if she was being judged by people who thought they were superior because they were already 'in,' because they were white, or because they had better clothing. She felt that she and her family were being criticized not for their character, but because they were different. The woman looked critically at the Mexicans standing along the wall, seeing all the differences between them and herself. The cloth of their clothes was of a courser weave; the color patterns and style of clothing were different. Their hairstyles were different. Their language was even a little different from the Spanish spoken by most of the Hispanics in the cafeteria that day. In addition, most of the people standing along the wall had been in the sun more. Their skin was a little darker than those who seemed to be judging them.

The Garzas could be understood and understand what was going on around them, but even the Hispanic Americans seemed to be communicating disapproval of the new arrivals through their glances and body language. Gaby and her brothers had never experienced this level of discrimination before, but they were determined not to show that they were bothered.

Finally, it was the Garzas' turn to visit with the registration clerk. It was plain to Gaby from the way the clerk looked at them, and the tone of disapproval in her voice, that she did not believe the Garza family belonged in the Weslaco school system. The clerk gave them a verbal list of the paperwork they needed to register but had not brought. The clerk's tone of voice and curt manner suggested that she believed they were trying to make her job difficult, that they should have known better, and that maybe they didn't bring their records intentionally to irritate her. Mrs. Garza had not known to bring the children's vaccination records; they also had no proof of residence, and the children did not have Social Security cards. All of the signs of rejection given by the clerk and others were very uncomfortable, but the greatest shock to Gaby was that she would have to start school in the fifth grade. The only answer she could get from the clerk when she asked, *"Por qué?"* was a curt and firm, "That's the way we do it." All other arguments and questions were simply ignored, and no justification was offered. A clerk at another table who had been watching the Garza predicament out of the corner of her eye said under her breath, *"Mejicanos pendejos!* (Stupid Mexicans!)" It was said loudly enough to be heard, but softly enough and anonymously enough to be denied.

The Garza family knew of no recourse, so they ignored the insult and went back home to regroup and gather what records they had. Birth certificates and other paperwork were found, and they visited the free clinic to get their vaccinations. No one believed they had had their immunizations in Mexico because they had no written proof, so all the Garza children got the full battery of vaccination shots appropriate to their ages—all in one visit.

The return trip to the huge registration center was a little better. There were not nearly as many people, and the clerk who had called them stupid was not in the room. The clerk who took their papers was white and seemed friendly. Gaby did not venture to dispute the mistake of her placement in fifth grade, assuming that the white person probably could not speak Spanish. She was not willing to risk the embarrassment she would feel at being able to speak only Spanish.

The question of Gaby's placement was not really addressed at registration, but her placement in fifth grade instead of seventh was because of the rules of one man. Due to the beginnings of high stakes testing in Texas, pressure was on districts to have their students perform well on the state tests. One man made the rule that students coming from another country and not fluent in English were to be placed in a grade below what they had achieved in their native country. That placement was made simply to assure that students were better able to pass the state tests. That man who made the rule also claimed to have school board policy behind him. No such policy existed, but the rule was enforced as if it did. That rule caused thousands of students to be placed below their achievement level with sometimes long-term negative results for the student. The district did well in comparison to other districts on the state testing scores, but very poorly in comparison to graduation rates among those same students. Often students placed a grade below their achievement, then held two years in that grade, simply left school out of frustration.

Gaby could not know at the time, but her placement was usual in Weslaco and most other border schools at the time. The unwritten policy was intended to make it easier for children to come into the school and learn English while studying familiar content so they could pass the state tests at lower grades. One practical piece of information missing in the making of this decision was understanding that the curriculum of almost any grade level in other countries was not the same as the curriculum of the United States. Most topics covered in seventh grade in the US had been taught in the lower grades in the Mexican schools. The curriculum of the seventh grade was not necessarily unfamiliar to Gaby and her cohorts from Mexico. In addition, the policy ignored the devastatingly derogatory effect that the placement had on the motivation of students to complete their schooling and graduate from high school. Significantly more Mexican-American students placed in lower grades, dropped out before completing high school as compared to a much smaller percent of those Mexican-American students not placed below their peers. That the policy was insulting and demeaning to recent immigrants was well understood by the man who made the rule, but he, and consequently the district, would not consider that his policy might be the cause of those students giving up on school. When anyone challenged this rule based on data, the man disregarded the research and argued that the students dropped out of school because of poverty, a lack of motivation, or a lack of early education—anything but his placement policy.

Gaby was forced by the policy to begin schooling as a fifth grader in Weslaco on the Sam Houston fifth and sixth-grade campus. She knew she was a year older than the average student beginning fifth grade, and she was highly insulted that her wonderful academic record was ignored when she was placed in fifth grade a second time. After all, she was the only student that had received Profesor Vargas' signature every year of her elementary education in Mexico, even though she was a year younger than her classmates. Insulted and depressed by the turn of events, Gaby reluctantly prepared to begin school in Texas.

FIRST DAY OF SCHOOL

Mr. and Mrs. Garza both accompanied Gaby to her first day of school. In Mexico, they did not feel the need to do this because the school was down the street a little ways and over one block. They knew Gaby's teacher and classmates, and she had been there before. She could not get lost. In this school system of many campuses with many buildings, full of strange people who looked at them as if they did not belong, they felt they needed to protect her through the first day.

So many parents drove their children to school and escorted them to class on the first day that the parking lot was full when the Garzas arrived. Both sides of the streets in all directions were lined with cars for several blocks. Finding a parking place was difficult, and they had to walk several blocks to the school. Gaby was late.

As it turned out, being late was the least of her difficulties that day. As the family neared the school, they saw that the campus was enclosed by a chain-link fence. The campus covered more than a city block. They walked up to the north side of the campus where there seemed to be no entrance. They walked around the perimeter of the fence, looking for an opening. They finally spied a large group of excited students and their parents entering the campus through a chain-link gate on the complete other side of the campus. The group seemed to know where they were going, so Gaby and her parents followed along. The chattering group ahead of them went through the gate, turned left along the inside of the fence, and entered a large flat-roofed building that turned out to be the school cafeteria. The air was heavy with the odors of strange food—at least the food odors were strange to Gaby. Gaby and her parents followed the crowd into the cafeteria, another very large room. The Weslaco Independent School District had such a high percentage of very poor students that breakfast was served to all students at no cost. All students at the Sam Houston fifth and sixth-grade campus were to meet in the cafeteria for breakfast, then separate into their classes from there.

The cafeteria was a very large room, much like the one at the junior-high campus where Gaby registered for school. The roof of the building was supported by large columns, and it seemed to be crammed full of students, parents, and the younger siblings of students.

Gaby found seats for them close to one of the support columns in the center of the room where they sat and waited. Soon, students left their parents and went out the doors in different directions, talking and laughing with friends. Occasionally a student looked Gaby's way while leaving. She felt that they must be laughing at her because she did not fit or know where to go. Finally, the parents of all the other children left the cafeteria through the doors they had entered, walked out the chain-link gate, got in their cars, and drove off. Gaby did not know where to go. Her parents did not know where to send her, and there seemed to be no one to ask, so they sat. Gaby felt lonely, scared, and sad. She sat between her worried and equally bewildered parents. Soon after the Garzas arrived, the cafeteria was empty except for them. Gaby did not eat breakfast because the food was strange. She could not identify the main course; all she knew was that it was some kind of flat bread that the students poured a thick brown liquid over before eating. She had never experienced pancakes.

Gaby did not want to leave the comfort of her parents, and they were reluctant to leave their only daughter in this strange place with people who might not treat her well. At the very least, they wanted to meet the teacher they would be trusting to take care of their little girl and stay with her through her first day. So, they sat, not knowing what to do or where to go to find help. The school in their village in Mexico did not have an office or clerks. If there was ever a problem, Mr. Vargas was in charge and solved the problem. The concept of a central administration was outside of their experience. The help that was available to them was not available, because they did not know about it. They did not know about principals, or principal's offices. They sat alone in a building that was almost as large as the entire campus in their beloved Ejido Buena Vista.

After what seemed like an eternity to Gaby, an office clerk walked into the cafeteria looking for a cup of coffee from the kitchen. On her way out of the room, she saw the girl and her parents sitting sadly alone. "Why don't you go to class?" she asked, but the question brought no response except a glance in her direction. She asked in Spanish, *"Por qué no va a su clase?"*

Standing and holding his cap in front of him, Mr. Garza spoke, *"No sabemos en donde esta la clase.* (We don't know where the class is.)"

The lady seemed to want to help. She asked what grade Gaby was to attend and, after commenting on her size for a fifth grader, took her around to a large red brick building and through several turns. They passed rooms full of children and finally arrived at a classroom she said was probably where Gaby belonged. The lady went inside and checked with the teacher. She found Gaby's name on the class roster then came back out to escort Gaby into the room, where she introduced her to Mrs. Lopez, Gaby's homeroom teacher for the school year. Gaby started crying at being taken from her parents. She did not resist or try to stay with them; she cried at the separation. Mr. and Mrs. Garza were not invited in, so they waited outside the room, looking worriedly through the windows. Mrs. Garza was wringing her hands, and tears were flowing down her cheeks. After Mrs. Lopez showed Gaby to a desk, she went outside to tell Gaby's parents that they must leave. She promised to take good care of Gaby and said she would make sure she was on the proper bus to get home.

Mrs. Lopez was a very pleasant middle-aged lady, short and plump with a quiet grandmotherly manner. Gaby immediately liked her and soon stopped crying, but she was still held in a deep sadness that she could not shake. She was in a class with little kids. In Buena Vista, she was the youngest; in Weslaco, she was the biggest student in the class and thought she must be the oldest. She was in a very strange and uncomfortable place. Everything Mrs. Lopez talked about in Spanish, she already knew. When Mrs. Lopez spoke in English, very little made sense to her. Gaby knew it was going to be a very bad year.

After a long and uncomfortable morning, the class took a break to go to the bathroom and freshen up for lunch. Gaby went to the bathroom and washed her hands. She *was* hungry. She thought that maybe if she got something good to eat, the day would not end as badly as it had begun. She made sure to keep someone from her class in sight so she would not get lost. In the cafeteria again, Gaby talked to no one but got in line for lunch with her class. The food was served on compartmentalized brown plastic trays. Most of the children already sitting in the cafeteria were eating the food and seemed to enjoy it, but nothing on her tray was familiar to Gaby. Hungry as she was, Gaby was also a picky eater. She did not eat any of the strange food. Even the milk was strange. She knew what it was, but she had never had milk with a meal. She had never seen milk in cartons. The milk she knew about came from a cow, not a paper carton.

No one seemed to notice or care that she did not eat any of her food. She followed a classmate to dispose of her leftover food and go to her afternoon class.

That first afternoon dragged by even more slowly than the morning. Gaby sat sadly in her seat and stared down at the desktop. She did not notice any of her fellow students, and they seemed uninterested in her. Gaby avoided eye contact. She was insulted and embarrassed to be attending fifth grade again after taking top honors in sixth grade the year before. In that moment, she did not want to be known, and she did not want to know any of the little kids she was being forced to call classmates.

Finally, the school day was over, and it was time to go home. Mrs. Lopez was as good as her word. She did her best to make Gaby comfortable and took her to the proper bus to get her home. On the way home on the bus, Gaby realized that finally her first day was over. It had been such a bad day, and she vowed not to go back. In her mind, she was surrounded by little children in a very strange place, had no friends, and was overwhelmed by the differences between La Escuela Salome' Gomez and the Sam Houston school, strikes one, two, and three. Gaby talked her fears and feelings over with her mother, begging to be allowed to stay home. Sanjuanita stroked Gaby's long hair with tears in her own eyes, knowing in her heart exactly how Gaby was feeling, but also knowing that her daughter was much stronger than she knew. She talked softly in accordance with her gentle manner, and convinced Gaby she would have to return to school the next day, and this time, she would have to ride the bus to school and get to class on her own. Not only could her mother not make the situation better, Gaby knew it would get worse.

SECOND DAY OF SCHOOL

The night after Gaby's first day in Weslaco schools, Gaby did not get much sleep. She had not yet gotten used to the house they were living in. The shadows moving in the room where the girls slept became monsters ready to grab her and carry her off to some horrible death. At one point, she had the thought that it might be best if one of the monsters in her imagination took her away. Any monster she could run into in her mind would be tame compared to the ones she was facing at her uncle's house and at school. Gaby decided that being carried away by some apparition would be an improvement over having to face the monster called school again the next day. With those thoughts swirling around in her brain, she finally fell asleep.

The next morning, after a good breakfast, Gaby steeled herself against what she must face. After tearfully kissing her mother good-bye, Gaby climbed sadly onto the bus with her primo and sat among the fifth and sixth-graders heading for Sam Houston Elementary School. She began preparing herself for her second day of her second round of fifth grade. She was resigned to do what she must, but it was plain to her that this fifth grade was not going to be anything like the fifth grade with Profesor Jose Jaime Vargas in his wonderful La Escuela Salome' Gomez. She wished to go back and see her beloved Profesor Vargas once again. But she knew what he would tell her. He would say, "Go and do your best." In her head, she could hear him saying the words, so she vowed that in his honor, she would do her best.

The bus dropped students off at Sam Houston Elementary at the back of the school. The drop-off point was the same as the pick-up point the afternoon before, but now she was facing the opposite direction. Gaby was again in an unfamiliar place, feeling lost, alone, and miserable. She did not recognize the school from this side and thought perhaps she had been left at the wrong place. She asked another student, "Es la Escuela Sam Houston?" The girl laughed and ran to join her friends. Being confused, ignored, and insulted caused Gaby to feel even more alone and out of place. She noticed that all the students seemed to be going to the same place, so she fought back tears, tried to swallow the lump in her throat, and followed them. Before school began the day before, everyone had gone to the big cafeteria for breakfast before going to classes. *Maybe that is the way it will be every day*, she thought to herself.

Gaby found the cafeteria and that food was being served, but she could not eat. Breakfast that morning was a serving of oatmeal, biscuits, milk, and two kinds of fruit juice. Gaby had never eaten oatmeal. She did not know what it was and was not willing to try strange food for the first time in a strange place. *Anyway, I have already had a good meal. I don't need this food*, she said to herself. To keep anyone from asking questions, she grabbed a couple of biscuits, sat down alone, and nibbled without truly eating. She sat alone and avoided eye contact with any other students.

The sound of the warning bell startled Gaby. Since she had been late to school the first day, she heard the bell only at the end of the day. This was something else Gaby was not familiar with and it caused her to be confused. It could not be the end of the day already. She wondered what the bell meant. Excited and chattering children started leaving the cafeteria in small groups. Gaby realized all of a sudden, that the bell was a signal for students to hurry to class. However, she did not remember the way to Mrs. Lopez' room. She had no group of students to follow; she did not recognize any of the students in the cafeteria from her class the day before. She had been so self-conscious and embarrassed the day before that she had not even looked at her classmates, nor had she noted the path from the cafeteria to Mrs. Lopez' classroom. Now, when she needed to find a classmate, she could not recognize a single one. No one came to her to say hello or show her to her class. So like the day before, Gaby stayed in the cafeteria. But on this second day, she was completely alone. Her parents were not with her. She sat in the cafeteria, feeling very frightened and lonely. Soon her throat hurt from her sadness, and tears began to run down her cheeks. She cried softly, not knowing what to do or where to find help.

After a time Mrs. Garcia, who worked in the school office, came through the cafeteria and saw Gaby sitting alone. "What are you doing here?" she asked. Gaby understood little English and spoke none. She sat without answering and looked into Mrs. Garcia's face. "Por qué no estas en la clase? (Why aren't you attending class?)" Gaby told her in Spanish that she did not know where she needed to go. "Quien es su maestra? (Who is your teacher?)" Gaby was so upset that she could not remember her teacher's name. "Ven conmigo. (Come with me.)" Gaby followed her to the office.

In the office, Mrs. Garcia asked Gaby about herself and asked about relatives that might live close by. She found out about Gaby's *primo*, Arturo, who was twelve and also in fifth grade. She called him into the office. Her cousin seemed to resent being disturbed by his *prima*—his ignorant, poor cousin who had invaded his home. He treated her with great disrespect in the office, talking down to her about her inability to speak English and laughing about her crying in the cafeteria and now in the office. He talked about where the Garza family lived and what Mr. Garza did for a living, making it sound as if the Garzas lived in poverty and were not worth the trouble they were going through in order to help her. Gaby began crying even harder. Mrs. Garcia could see that calling the cousin in to assist was not helpful. She scolded him for being so cruel and sent him back to class then looked in her files for Gaby's schedule. "Ah, here you are," she said as she pulled out a sheet of paper. She gave Gaby time to wash her face and gather herself before she escorted her to Mrs. Lopez' classroom.

On this morning of bad events, one more shock was waiting for Gaby. Finally safe in the proper room with Mrs. Lopez making her feel as if they had been expecting her and waiting for her to begin the day, a girl named Sandra Alvarado looked at her and asked, "Do you want to sit next to me?" Gaby sat in the desk next to Sandra. Sandra shared her pencil, paper, and other supplies, because Gaby had come with nothing. When it became necessary, Sandra showed her to the girls' bathroom. Feeling safer, and therefore curious, Gaby began looking around at her classmates besides Sandra. She figured that it might be handy to be able to spot one of them in the cafeteria in case she did not remember the way to class the next day as well. There across the room smiling at her was Claudia Patricia Davalos Alvarado! Claudia had been her greatest competition in fourth grade at La Escuela Salome' Gomez and her best friend in Buena Vista. This was a mixed blessing. Claudia was a friend, but she was also very smart and could again be her greatest competition for the teacher's signature at the end of the year. *Would Mrs. Lopez hold the same competition?* Gaby wondered, almost hoping she wouldn't. In spite of her sadness and anxiety about being thrust into this new place, Gaby began to feel the old desire to be the best in class. Inside, she was beginning to rise to the challenge of this new school. Remembering Señor Vargas was giving her a confidence she had not felt since leaving Mexico. Her impending competition with Claudia, and her silent promise to Profesor Vargas to do her best, began to have an impact on her outlook. Suddenly, Gaby began to sit up a little straighter, listen a little closer, and look around the room for clues to the lessons she would have to learn.

DISCONTENT IN FIFTH GRADE

Mrs. Lopez was a good teacher. She was very kind and considerate toward her children. *She is kind of like a second mother or an abuela*, Gaby thought. She seemed to be very interested in her students. Teaching them to speak, read, and write in English were her primary goals for the year. But she moved the class very slowly so that even the slowest learner could keep up. Gaby often thought, *You have to move on! I am getting sleepy!* But she would never say such a thing to Mrs. Lopez because that would be dis-respectful. Omar was an older boy in the class who seemed to intentionally keep the class moving slowly. Gaby was often angry with him for playing around instead of paying attention. She tried to be patient, but there came a time when she began to make moves to help herself.

A NEW HOME

Concentrating on her studies became easier after September 16, 1990, when the Garza's moved into their new home that Gaby's dad and uncles built for them. It was a two-room house; one room served as the kitchen and dining area. They even had a couch in the living area. The other room was separated into two parts by a curtain to allow Gaby and her brothers their 'room' and the other side of the curtain was her parents' 'room.' It was small compared to the house they had lived in on the ranch in Mexico, but in spite of the lack of room, Gaby felt it was a lot better than living with the relatives. Just like they had in Mexico, the new home had an outhouse and a small separate room filled with pails of water to serve as a shower room. They didn't have running water inside the house, so the dishes had to be washed on a table on the back porch. Their lifestyle didn't change much, but it was still difficult to adapt to the new area, the new neighbors, the new language, and the new school. However, it was a doubly big day as Mexicans celebrate Independence Day on September sixteenth. It is called Diez y Seis. The Garza family felt they were obtaining another kind of independence. Now, they had their family privacy. Sanjuanita made a special dinner to celebrate, and everyone promised to take good care of their new home.

The first two years the Garzas lived in their new home, they were constantly hiding behind locks. The neighborhood was full of gangs and other dangers. They had no desire to play outside or get to know the neighbors. Sanjuanita employed her time cleaning the house, cooking, and sewing new clothing for the children. Gaby and her brothers   spent most of their time at home, studying and playing games inside the house. During homework time, Sanjuanita still sat with the children to make sure they were doing their work. She expressed her frustration at not being able help her children in anything other than math. Sanjuanita could not read or write the new language, so that all she could do was watch her children struggle with their work. She comforted Gaby many times while she cried wrestling with homework. Gaby felt overwhelmingly lost most of the time, and much of that time, her dictionary was her only help. She dedicated most of her free time to reading and writing the new language.

LEARNING ENGLISH FROM RANDY

To begin to help herself, Gaby asked Mrs. Lopez, "Can I sit with someone that speaks English?" The next day her frustration peaked, she restated her desire: "I want to learn to read in English." Mrs. Lopez had come to realize that Gaby was unusually committed to learning and desired more than she was getting. She began giving Gaby projects. Gaby painted plaster-of-paris pumpkins, and colored and cut decorations for Thanksgiving. She was given other tasks too, but all of them seemed to be busywork to

Gaby and did not teach her any English. She could easily do the extra artsy jobs and still keep up with the instruction in class, but she was not learning to read in English, at least not as quickly as she wanted. Finally Gaby asked to be sent to the library to learn to read faster. She picked up simple picture books and made a game of trying to figure out what the words on the pages meant by analyzing the pictures. Mrs. Lopez finally got Gaby a partner to read with. Her partner was a freckle-faced boy named Randy White who agreed to sit with her and teach her to read in English. That plan was just fine with Gaby. The fifth grade content was not a challenge, so she kept her focus on learning English.

At the library, Gaby would sit with Randy, and together they entered into a painstaking process of teaching and learning English from books. She would attempt to read a line from a book. Randy would correct her pronunciation, and then translate the sentence into Spanish so she could understand the meaning of the words. Gaby would often take time out from the book to ask questions that were personal or cultural in nature, and most of the time Randy would patiently try to explain. Gaby wanted to know if his freckles hurt, why he cut his hair so that it was longer in the back than in the front, and why his hair was red. She asked why children in the US did not want to learn, and why she was being treated the way she was by the school even though she wanted very badly to learn. There were many more "whys" she did not understand that Randy could not explain. Gaby's questioning often strained the relationship. At times Randy would get defensive and call her ugly names. On these occasions, she would become stubborn and not cooperate with his "teaching."

This somewhat friendly but often stormy relationship lasted four or five weeks. The end came during the reading of a children's book about ducks. Gaby had read a line, and Randy asked her in Spanish to pronounce the word "every" in English, pointing to it in the book. She refused and asked him to pronounce it. Secretly, she was sure she would pronounce it badly and did not want to give him any excuse to laugh at her. She was determined to not be embarrassed. She knew she had heard the word, but reading it did not make sense, because the second "e" in "every" made no sound. Spanish words were very predictable once you knew the rules, but English seemed to not have very many consistent rules, and most words seemed to break the rules anyway. Randy gently demanded she say it first, and again she refused, saying he was the teacher and had to say it first. He came back a little stronger with his demand, saying that since he was the teacher, she had to do as he told her. They sent the argument back and forth several more times. Randy remained insistent, and Gaby remained stubborn. Finally Randy said, "I don't want to teach you anymore." He picked up his belongings and left. That was Gaby's last lesson from Randy. Randy had given up on her.

In spite of the personal turmoil, Randy gave her a really good start into learning to read, write, and pronounce English. She started checking books out from the library on a regular basis and would use a Spanish/English dictionary to translate, and an English dictionary to figure out the proper pronunciation. Sometimes it would take her weeks to finish reading a single book, but she *would* finish. She wouldn't understand everything that she was reading, especially because when translating English to Spanish the structures of the sentences are almost always backward. She liked to say that the English language was backward, but Randy would correct her. All she wanted to accomplish was to read and speak the language so that she could move to an all-English class and not remain in a bilingual class. Randy helped her, and she was grateful to him, even though they did not separate on good terms.

ALL-ENGLISH CLASS

When she next saw Mrs. Lopez after Randy stopped teaching her, Gaby made her demand: "I want to go to an all-English class! I want to learn something new!" After the paperwork went back and forth for signatures of Gaby's parents, Mrs. Lopez reluctantly arranged for Gaby to attend another class at the school that would be taught completely in English.

At the beginning of her new class, Gaby wondered about her decision to be immersed in English. She felt totally lost in the new language. She did not understand anything but a word or two here and there, and certainly not enough to make sense of instructions or abstract concepts. Regardless, she struggled on through January and February. Gradually she caught on to the schedule, the system, and the predictable procedures and requirements of the classroom, and most importantly, she began to associate the vocabulary that was used to signal these systemic events. She quickly learned the requirements of spelling and vocabulary and began consistently making hundreds on all of those assignments. Math became very easy, because she had already learned all the concepts for fifth grade in La Escuela Salome'

Gomez. Understanding the directions for most of the assignments was not necessary, because the language of arithmetic is international and not verbal. The class had not yet gotten deep into word problems. In her new class, she eventually received more help with her English. Gaby met Benita, a new friend who helped her. Benita was in her 'regular' all-English class and fluent in both English and Spanish. Benita helped her often with pronunciation and meaning of unfamiliar words. Gaby helped herself considerably by going to the library often to check out books. Every day after school, Gaby waited in the library, reading and studying until her bus arrived.

PHYSICAL EDUCATION

One of Gaby's most difficult classes was physical education. The female PE coach embarrassed all the girls by telling them to ignore that their breasts would move up and down when they ran. She also told them to keep running, even though they may stain their panties when they were having their monthly flow. Some would refuse to run in front of the boys or run at all when they were having their monthly flow. The coach was trying to get them to run in spite of their embarrassment or their discomfort. Of course, there were some girls who would run proudly, hoping to be noticed by the boys and Mr. Casas, the male PE coach. Gaby had noticed that he was young, athletic, and good-looking. All the girls had noticed.

The first time the coaches required students to run the perimeter of the playground, Gaby's old malady showed itself. After almost completing the first lap, she fainted. When she woke up, she was living the earnest dream of most of the fifth and sixth grade girls at Sam Houston Elementary School. Mr. Casas had her in his arms and was carrying her to a cool place. Several times that fall during strenuous exercise, Gaby fainted in the PE class. Finally, Coach Casas assigned her to do 'exercises' in a cool classroom during PE class time. She would report to class, answer for roll call, then go to the room where Mr. Casas had a video player set up. Instead of exercising, she watched *The Goonies* movies and practiced her English.

Gaby completed fifth grade with all A's on her report card and was expecting to go on to sixth grade the next year. She had proven that she could do everything necessary to pass and even excel in the fifth grade. Weslaco ISD schools had other ideas. There was an unwritten policy developed by the same man that required the placement of children from Mexico one grade below their achievement in Mexico. The policy included that children who did not speak English fluently at the beginning of their first year in Weslaco schools, must not only be placed in the grade below the last grade they had completed in another country, but they must spend two years or until they become fluent in English in that same grade. There was a test on the English language that any student in Gaby's situation had to pass in order to be considered for promotion. To be allowed to take the test, a student had to be recommended by their teacher. Gaby was not recommended. Of course, the school had neglected to tell the Garza family about this policy at the beginning of the school year. At the time Gaby felt she should be going to the eighth grade she would not even be allowed to progress to the sixth grade. Now used to being insulted by the 'rules' of the district, Gaby accepted the situation with a degree of resignation.

FIFTH GRADE AGAIN

In Mexico, Gabriela had gone to school through the month of June and started back in the middle of August. Summer break in Texas was about the same. The summer of 1991 was uneventful and boring for Gaby. She spent most of her waking hours watching the Public Broadcast Station in English. Her younger brothers, Gamaliel and German, played with each other, leaving Gaby to her own devices. Through the day, they all waited expectantly for Papi to come home from work. That was when he worked days. During that summer, Papi worked the swing shift at his job at a sugar mill, meaning that one week he worked through the day, the next week he worked at night. When he worked nights, the family spent the day whispering and making as little noise as possible so they did not wake up Papi.

Once each week, the family would take a trip to Carl's Grocery store or to Valley Mart to buy groceries. The family continued to be somewhat confused by the differences in foods between Mexico and the US. They were not used to white potatoes, flour with the fine texture people demand in the US, or white chicken eggs. Gaby thought white eggs did not look like they could possibly be healthy to eat. But the most confusion came from the change in currency. Mrs. Garza could not get accustomed to the idea of four quarters to a dollar, five pennies to a nickel, and twenty nickels to a dollar. Nothing matched the base ten currency with which she was familiar in Mexico.

Finally the long summer was over, and it was time to register for school again. A *tio* (uncle) from her father's family took Gaby and her brothers to take care of school registration. Gamaliel was assigned to go to Airport Elementary and Gaby was to attend Louise Black for fifth grade again. District attendance lines had been moved.

Mr. Handy was Gaby's new homeroom and science teacher. For language arts, her teacher was Mrs. Cardenas. She soon learned to love all her teachers and made even better grades than she had in fifth grade at Sam Houston Elementary. She was easily the top student of her class.

10

Growing and Changing

FIRST LOVE

November 7 of her second year in fifth grade in the US, Gaby celebrated her thirteenth birthday. She wasn't the tallest girl in class, but she knew she was the eldest. She was more developed and had different interests than most other students. One of those interests was boys. She never confessed to her mother how young she was when her stomach first filled with butterflies and her heart leapt because of a boy, but it all started the first day of fifth grade at the Louise Black campus. She was just starting school in Mrs. Cardenas classroom when Guadalupe was brought in by the principal's secretary. He had a nosebleed, which he later explained was caused by a fist-fight. Mrs. Cardenas seated him in front of Gaby. In that moment, Gaby thought she was the luckiest girl in the entire world. Guadalupe Ibarra was tall and slender and had gorgeous eyes, of the same deep blue of her father's.

One day at recess, Gaby saw Guadalupe again bleeding from his nose. He took the Kleenex she offered him and pressed it on his face to soak up the blood. "I was just in another fight," he said simply. "I can tell," was her curt response. She sat down beside him and they talked through recess almost immediately becoming good friends. From that day forward, Guadalupe and Gaby were inseparable at school. Guadalupe was also an older student. He was Gaby's age. He was in fifth grade because he had failed, not because he was from Mexico, but he was kind to her and a good conversationalist. The two often met at recess, sat together on the bus, and would keep each other company at school dances. Gaby gave him her heart and never took it back. Much later, in high school, Guadalupe would break her heart, but he was still her first love.

SAME GRADE, THIRD VERSE

During Gaby's second year of fifth grade in the US, and her third round of fifth grade altogether, she mostly played in Mr. Handy's science class yet still passed with an A. All the topics had been taught to her by Profesor Vargas in La Escuela Salome' Gomez, but there were still challenges when it came to the English language. Once Mrs. Cardenas, seeing Gaby's talent and drive, gave her the assignment of reading Charlotte's Web and demanded a written summary. Gaby spent considerable time copying sentences and paragraphs from the book, and when completed, she turned this in as her "summary." Mrs. Cardenas returned the paper covered in red marks. Gaby was hurt. She had worked so hard, and she had never before gotten a paper back from a teacher stating that she had failed. Mrs. Cardenas stated simply when asked, "This is not a summary."

"Well then, what is a summary?" asked Gaby. "Look at the back of the book. That synopsis is too short, but it is a kind of summary. To do a summary, you tell the important parts of a story in your own words." Gaby took the book and her paper and did the assignment again. When she turned it in to Mrs. Cardenas, she was not expecting anything but a nod of agreement that the latest paper was indeed a summary. Instead, Mrs. Cardenas took the paper to grade. It came back with a score of 100 percent and a congratulatory note, very much like one Profesor Vargas would have written.

It was in Mrs. Cardenas' class that Gaby was first introduced to Scholastic books. She was hooked on reading in English from then on. Seldom would one find Gaby with a free moment without a book in her hand or at least close by. By the end of her second year in American fifth grade, Gaby was almost fluent in English and had distinguished herself as a scholar to her teachers, again making A's in all her classes. She was recommended for the language-proficiency test and would finally be allowed to progress to the sixth grade.

SIXTH GRADE

The summer of 1992 was as hot and boring to Gaby as the previous summer had been. It went very much like the summer of 1991, and when she and her brothers again registered for classes, Gaby was anxious to begin school again. The district had undergone more changes, and she was assigned, along with all other sixth graders of the district, to the new Mary Hoge campus. It was a huge building intended to house over a thousand students under one roof. Her principal was to be Mrs. Pullian, and her teachers would include Mr. Arnold for language arts; these were people who would soon become very important to her life.

The new Mary Hoge campus had a different structure than the other campuses Gaby had been on; once inside, she seldom had to walk outside until the end of the school day. There were other, more important differences. Gaby could not be sure what the underlying plan for the structure was, but it certainly worked well for her. The campus held sixth, seventh, and eighth graders. Some classes, like health, had students from all three grades mixed together. She often found herself in classes with seventh and eighth graders. She noticed that the eighth graders in her classes were doing the same work she was doing, and she was getting the same or better grades than they were. She knew the system was doing something odd to her, but this experience showed her that she could perform at least at the same level as students who were two grades above her. She began to revisit the difference between where she was, sixth grade, and ninth grade, where she felt she should be. It was apparent to her that eighth graders were not operating at a different level than she was. She knew she could do the same work, and just as well, as the students she saw in the eighth grade. She began to form the notion that she could and should be with those eighth-graders when they went to high school. *How can I get the school to move me to ninth grade in the fall?* This question was now constantly bouncing around in her mind throughout the school days and often into the night. She planned and schemed, then discarded the plans and schemes, but came up with new ones.

Finally, a plan began to form in Gaby's mind, and her confidence was now such that she felt she could achieve her objective if she could only get some help. If she was successful, she would be in ninth grade the following year. While she should be attending tenth grade, she understood the nature of high school. No one could start high school in the tenth grade. She was dedicated to making her plan work. Yet she could not have known that there were other forces coming into play that would put the right people into her life at this critical moment to help make it possible to fulfill her plan.

11

Meeting Gaby, Forming a Plan

PESTERING THE TEACHERS

"Please, Mr. Arnold, I need to be in the ninth grade next year."
The adjectives Gabriela's sixth-grade teachers would use to describe their year with her would most likely be "stellar" and "annoying." She had no grade average lower than ninety-five percent in any of her classes. All her teachers were proud of her accomplishments and appreciated both her demonstrations of great respect for them and her love for learning anything and everything they taught. She seemed an insatiable learner and a very able student. Her teachers worked hard to challenge her without ever feeling they had really seen the extent of her abilities or fully challenged her work ethic. However, almost from the beginning of the year, she insisted that she should be placed in the ninth grade the following year and asked each of her teachers to help her accomplish her goal.

"Mr. Arnold, I'm fourteen. The other fourteen-year-olds are about to start ninth grade. That is what I want. I want to be in the ninth grade next year."

"Gaby, no one has ever moved two grades in one year—at least no one that I know of. We can probably get you over seventh grade in time to start eighth, but ninth? I don't believe that will be allowed, even if you could do it."

"Won't you at least try? Mr. Arnold, please help me. Won't you at least let me talk to the person who makes that decision? Let me change their mind."

"Gaby, I'm not sure I even know who would make that decision." Seeing the determination on her face, and knowing from personal experience with her that she would not give up, he finally relented, "Okay. I'll try."

PRIOR EFFORTS

When she first came to Texas from Mexico two years before, Gabriela could not speak, read, or write the English language. She understood a little, but not confidently. At the end of two years in fifth grade, her reading, speaking, and writing abilities in English all reflected excellent fluency and were of a quality to be admired. More importantly, she had gained a degree of self-confidence and retained her stubbornness from her younger days with Papi.

Standard practice for Weslaco ISD, and most other schools in Texas that regularly received students from Mexico, was and is to start a non-English speaker in a grade one year behind their age, and then only promote them at the end of the first year if they have achieved a high measure of fluency. The intent is to give students time to learn the new language before entering junior high or high school. The belief was that they would learn English faster while studying curriculum to which they had already been exposed. However, like most government decisions intended for the greater good, the ultimate effect of the practice is largely negative. Placing non-English speaking students in classes with much younger students, then not allowing them to progress regardless of their efforts, defeats all but the most determined of recent immigrants. This practice violates and dishonors who a person is and where they come from. It also negates and discounts what they have academically accomplished up to that point. The insidious underlying philosophy is that, whatever they have learned and whatever they have accomplished to the point of entry into the United States is of no value. Children treated in this manner see themselves as victims of the system or 'less than' those who were lucky enough to be born here. They are forced to either stand up against a formidable system and fight for themselves or simply lie down and give up any sense of accomplishment in school.

Most people when faced with being violated by an enormous system will resign themselves to their fate and lie down taking the easier route of being a victim. Most children do not have a developed sense of justice, or their confidence is so low that they don't realize they have the option of fighting for themselves. Most parents of immigrant children are not well educated and are very happy and satisfied that their children can even go to school. Most will go along with whatever notion is proposed in the name of helping the child, no matter how misguided or nonsensical the proposal. Children see this treatment very differently than their parents. Many children treated in this manner drop out of school rather than attend classes with children two or three years younger with no apparent way to progress more quickly and catch up to their peers. Thusly insulted, some mentally drop out even though they are still physically in attendance, then they silently leave whenever the opportunity presents itself. They do not march in protest or sue the school system, they simply drop out, and by age sixteen they are no longer in the system. A large percent of these students drop out between eighth and ninth grade to go to work in the fields for very low wages. They accept a low position in society and work hard at what jobs they can find, hoping for a better future for their children. The children and their parents reason that even with the inequities they suffer, what they have in the US is far better than what they have come from, so they settle for less than what they could have. Gaby was not one to settle or give up easily.

PAPI'S PLAN

Gabriela's mother also went against the norm. Though she was a very quiet and submissive wife, she had an inner strength that would never fail her children. She was determined to see her boys complete school and secretly hoped the same for her daughter. She showed great respect for education and would move mountains to see that her children were free from the life of drudgery and uncertainty she and Beto had known all their lives. In a few weeks, young Gilberto, Gabriela's older brother, would graduate. Her desire was that Gilberto would be only the first of her children to complete school successfully; he was to be the one to point the way. Beto farmed other people's land along the US border, while his own land lay fallow or was worked by young Gilberto on his visits to Mexico. He saw the benefit of educating his boys. Beto agreed his sons should graduate from high school and go on to more schooling, establishing careers in the United States. He did not see the same future for his daughter.

Gaby overheard many discussions between her Papi and young Gilberto concerning his future. She hoped her parent's aspirations extended to her, and she wished to fulfill them as soon as possible. She was in a hurry to get to college. She dreamed of college and where it would lead her. Gaby felt Papi did not value an education for her. He never talked with her concerning the future. However, every time she heard her brother talk of his plans to go on to higher education, Gaby entered the dream herself. She was convinced she would go to college. In fact all other considerations were crowded out of her mind, but her father seemed to have no such plans for her.

ASK THE PRINCIPAL

The principal, Mrs. Pullian, answered, "Gabriela, you are a good student, but even good students have limitations. We could consider helping you skip seventh grade to begin eighth grade next fall. There would be tests to take and pass, of course, but to skip seventh and eighth grade in the same summer? No, no one has done it, and I won't approve it. Socially it would be a disaster."

"But, Mrs. Pullian," Gaby reasoned, "the students completing eighth grade this year are my age. Ninth grade is where I belong. How can that be a disaster?" Mrs. Pullian was a good principal and worked hard for her students, but she was very adamant in her answer to Gaby's request, and not willing to negotiate. Mrs. Pullian was very stubborn once her mind was made up. No amount of logic or emotion would prevail. Once she had said, "No," Mrs. Pullian would not change her mind easily. Gaby soon realized that she could not depend on help from Mrs. Pullian to reach ninth grade by fall.

"Mrs. Pullian, I mean no disrespect, but is there someone else I can talk to?"

"No, not that I know of. But you can try. You can talk to anyone you please. It will not hurt or offend me in any way. However, so far as I know, the final decision is mine."

Gaby left the office disappointed, but thinking, *She did give me permission to talk to anyone else I want. There has to be someone. Mr. Arnold probably knows.*

ASK PAPI?

In sixth grade, Gaby was already very emotionally invested in going to college. However, her wrestling with the district over her placement had caused her to doubt that anyone would listen to her desires. Those doubts extended to concerns about the plans her parents might have for her. After all, she had not heard them talk of her and college in the same conversation. Fearing the worst, she had become too afraid to address the question with her father. She often talked about it to German. Because he was so young he did not understand; it was almost like talking to herself. Casper sat and smiled and held on to the sister he adored whenever she talked of college. He hugged her close and tried to comfort her when she cried out of frustration. He did not understand anything except that Gaby wanted something as badly as she wanted to breathe, but it seemed she felt the dream was hopeless. He felt that she had made the right decision when she finally determined that she must talk to her father. In her family, as in most Mexican families, fathers had the last word on every subject. Beto's word was final. If he said no to college, she would not go to college.

She rehearsed her speech to the father she loved and respected many times, but she remained fearful of his response. She felt that she must be very careful to bring the subject up to him at just the right time and in just the right way. For several days, she made her speech to the mirror or Casper, imagining her father's response. Each day she revised the speech and tried it again. She decided an immediate yes would probably be too much to expect. "I'll think about it. Ask me again later," would be a victory. An indefinite answer could give her something to argue from if he later said no. However, when she saw it in her mind, his answer was always no. When she got to that part of the conversation in her mind, her stomach would begin to hurt. One thing she thought might buy her some grace with her father was being recognized as a good student. *Maybe if the school will let me skip to the class I should be in, just maybe, Papi will see that I should go to college.* The speech and question would have to wait for her to convince the school to allow her to begin high school next fall.

Of all her teachers, Mr. Arnold, her language arts teacher, seemed to be the kindest and most willing to help. He was the one who made the appointment for her with Mrs. Pullian. Now Gaby pushed him again. "Surely someone will listen. Who can I talk to? Who is Mrs. Pullian's boss?"

Mr. Arnold promised to look for someone. However, he told her he was convinced she could not jump that far ahead, so he began looking for someone who could convince Gaby that it was not possible for any student to move from the sixth to the ninth grade. His reason for looking for someone to tell Gaby "no" was twofold. First, he truly believed that the move would not be good for Gaby. She would miss too much socialization. Second, it went against any sort of tradition. Skipping one grade was rare in Weslaco ISD; skipping two had never been done to his or Mrs. Pulliam's knowledge, and Mrs. Pulliam had been in the district for many years. In education, as in almost all regulated institutions, especially in the early 1990s, if something had not been done before, it simply wasn't to be done at all. The usual response was that the decision was, "for the good of the student." An educator had to become a turtle, willing to stick out his or her neck, in order to do innovative things. Weslaco ISD did not reward innovation, especially if it was at the request of a student.

12

I Get A Call

Late in March, 1993, I was in my office dutifully conducting the business of executive director of secondary education when I received a call from within the district.

"Hello, this is Dufner."

"Dr. Dufner, this is Mr. Arnold, a sixth-grade language arts teacher at the middle school."

"Yes, Mr. Arnold, I know who you are. What can I do for you?"

"Well, Dr. Dufner, I have a big favor to ask of you. Will you come and talk to one of my students?"

"Sure. What shall I talk about, and who is the student?"

"I have a student who wants to go to ninth grade next year. Her name is Gabriela; she is fourteen and, at her age, should be beginning ninth grade, except that she came to the US nearly three years ago and was placed in fifth grade then retained for another year. She wants to go to ninth grade next year. We've already talked to Mrs. Pullian. Mrs. Pullian told her she would not approve anyone skipping two grades at once. The trouble is, Gaby keeps bugging me about it, and I need someone with some clout to come and put an end to the idea. I need you to talk to her and convince her that she cannot move (ahead) two grades. At least, I want the argument to be in your court instead of mine. She asks me about it nearly every day. Since you are the Executive Director of Secondary Education, maybe she will listen to you."

"Why was she retained?"

"Because that is what we do. A student who comes to Weslaco from Mexico and does not speak English well is placed in a grade below what they have completed in their native country, or a grade below their age-mates, then they are usually kept for two years in that grade so their language skills can catch up. Her grades were good enough to pass even at the end of her first time in fifth. In fact they were very good. In sixth grade, her grades are tops in every class. She is difficult to challenge with our curriculum focused on the Texas Educational Assessment of Minimum Skills."

I paused for a few moments to think. I don't know why I answered as I did. I had never had this question in front of me, but after some thought, I said, "Mr. Arnold, I can't promise to tell her that she can or cannot skip two grades. At least I can't without talking to her and her teachers and, I guess, finding out about whether there is a policy that covers this problem. I will grant that I haven't heard of anyone doing that, but I also don't know of any rule against it. What I need to know immediately is if she were to be skipped to ninth grade, would she have the academic strength and the commitment to handle the work?"

"I don't have a good feel for ninth-grade curriculum," Mr. Arnold responded confidently," but I know she will eat seventh grade alive. She is the best student I have ever taught. She reads, she does her homework, she studies, she discusses things in class at a very high level, and she asks questions that I can't answer. From my perspective, sir, she is the perfect student."

"Alright," I answered. "Today is Friday. Let me check the calendar. How about I come to the school on Wednesday during your class period to talk to her?"

"Well, at ten thirty she will be in PE. That would be a better time. She wouldn't miss any class time."

"Okay, ten thirty it is. Can you take care of the logistics and get her to me somewhere on campus where we can talk?"

"Yes, sir. That will be fine. I will get her out of class to discuss this with you. She'll meet you in the library. At least this should buy me a couple of days' peace."

"Fine, Mr. Arnold. By the way, just so I know, what is the student's full name?"

"Garza, Gabriela Garza."

"Okay, tell Gabriela I will talk with her. I will see her on Wednesday at ten thirty at the campus library."

"Great! Good-bye, Dr. Dufner, and thanks."

I had been working long hours to transition from the executive director of secondary education to the fifth principal of Cuellar Junior High in four years. I was pretty much at the end of the tasks I had to complete before moving to Cuellar, so I was confident I could spend a little time on Gaby's concern. Looking her name up in the database, I discovered that Gabriela was scheduled to be a Cuellar Junior High seventh-grade student the next year. The fact that I would be her principal and charged with her education for seventh and eighth grades gave me a little leverage if I needed it.

After looking up Gabriela's placement, attendance, and grades on the computer, I was very impressed, but I gave the conversation with Mr. Arnold little thought until I saw the appointment on my calendar the next Wednesday morning. The Friday afternoon before, however, I did bring the topic up to the outgoing director of reading, the man who made the rules governing the placement of elementary students from Mexico. His unofficial rules were what had caused Gaby and hundreds of other recent immigrants to be placed with younger students. His opinion was that no student should be placed with their peers until they had a command of the English language. According to him, if a student was not fluent in English, they should be considered to have failed, regardless of their grades. In prior discussions with him, I had pointed out that students who were placed in lower grades by the system had not failed, they had simply not been given the opportunity to succeed and those were two very different things. After these discussions, he generally walked away in a huff, saying that the rules had been approved by the board and would not change. Obviously he was defensive of his rule and because he was leaving the district shortly to begin a professorship, he did not want to discuss the issue. Looking further into district policy records, I found no such actual policy on the books.

MEETING GABY

Five minutes before we were set to meet, Gaby walked haltingly into the school library, looking around nervously and carrying a stack of papers hugged to her chest. I was already seated at a table between the stacks in the research section of the library. The school set of Encyclopedia Britannica's were at my right hand.

Gaby was obviously from Mexico. The respectful attitude she had been taught to hold toward her elders had not faded, and her style of dress and braids were almost sure signs of having lived in Mexico. She had a dark complexion and jet-black hair with a quiet beauty and an air of purpose that was not totally overshadowed by her nervousness. Her physical development and apparent feminine grace were far beyond the average sixth-grader.

"Are you Dr. Dufner?"

"Yes, I am. Are you Gabriela Garza?"

"I'm Gaby. Dr. Dufner, will you move me to ninth grade next year?" She wasted no time getting to the point of our meeting.

"Well, Gaby, that *is* what I came to discuss with you. Why don't you sit down and tell me about yourself and tell me why you are in such a hurry to graduate that you want to skip from sixth to ninth grade."

"When I came from Mexico, I should have been starting seventh grade. They put me in fifth. Then, even though my grades were very good, they placed me in fifth again the next year. You see, I should really be starting tenth grade next year, but skipping three grades might be too much, and I know about credits in high school."

"Gaby, I'm a little confused in the math. Mr. Arnold told me that you are fourteen, and your records show you are fourteen. Fourteen is the age when most people start ninth grade. How is it that you should be in tenth?"

"I skipped kindergarten. I started in first grade when I was five."

"Okay, how did you do in school in Mexico?"

"I was at the top of my class. I got Profesor Vargas' signature each year. Every year I have been at the top of my class, except for a little time right after I came from Mexico. Mr. Vargas, my teacher at my school in Ejido Buena Vista, gave a certificate to the top student of each grade every year.

He signed the paper. Every year I worked hard to get that signature. Here, I have many certificates that show I am a good student." She showed me several certificates with her name printed in the middle and a signature with a flourish at the bottom. I could not read the signature, but assumed it was genuine.

"Do you understand why you were placed in fifth grade and then retained?"

"No. They said it was because I did not speak English well. They wanted me to learn English while studying things I already knew. That does not make sense. Why study the solar system all over again? All you learn is different words for the same things you already know—then they make you do it twice? I was treated like I was not a good student, like I was stupid, but I already knew most of the things we studied twice in fifth grade because Profesor Vargas was my teacher. He knows almost everything, and he taught me for six years."

"Mr. Arnold tells me you are a very able student."

"Yes. I like school, and I like learning. I have always been the top of my class."

"What is your best class?"

"If you mean what class do I do the best in, I don't have one. I do very well in all of them. If you mean what class do I like the best, language arts, because Mr. Arnold lets me answer with my thoughts instead of only demanding that I repeat *his* thoughts."

"Why do you want to be in ninth grade next year? Wouldn't it be easier to just continue to seventh?"

"I can do the work. Easier does not mean I am learning. There is so much to learn, and I can learn much faster than I am being taught. I can read my brother's books from high school, and I can understand them. Ninth grade should be easier than his work. He is about to graduate from high school."

"Gaby, moving two grades is a big commitment. Even if it were allowed, there will be a lot of reading and many tests to pass before both grades can be completed. Are you sure you can commit to something that big?"

"I don't know how much work it will be, but I will do whatever you assign. I will work hard, and I will complete the work. I promise I will not quit until it is finished."

At this point, I was very impressed with Gaby's presence, her scholarship, her common sense, and the fire in her belly to succeed. Without realizing it, I had already made the decision to be on her team, but working in a highly political system, I knew to proceed carefully. Educational systems are as political as any system on earth. If you make a wrong move at the wrong time, your career is over. Protocols must be observed, and the hierarchy must be honored. I had to have all my ducks in a row. First I had to make sure that what she was proposing would be legal. I suspected it would be, but knowledge is power, and in Weslaco ISD, power is everything.

"I'll tell you what, Gabriela, I will call the Texas Education Agency to find out what rules or laws we may be thinking about breaking. If I see that this may be possible, I will bring books and copies of class curriculum requirements to you for each course you will have to master in order to skip seventh and eighth grade. Give me until next Monday at ten thirty, and we'll meet right back here. If it is legal, and you are willing to do the work, we will begin to develop a plan to get this done."

"Thank you, Dr. Dufner. I am willing to do the work." Smiling, she started to leave.

"Not so fast, Gaby. There is a caveat." "What is that? What is a caveat?"

"In this case, it means there is another requirement that you must meet before Monday."

"Anything. I'll do whatever you want."

"Gabriela, you and I cannot make this decision without the knowledge and consent of your parents. I want you to talk to your parents about this before Monday. If they say no, we cannot proceed. Do you understand?"

"Is this a state rule?"

"No, this is my rule."

"Yes, sir. I will talk to them."

Sensing the answer to my question, I asked, "You have not talked to your father about this idea, have you?"

"No, sir. I have not."

"You must, Gaby. I will not proceed, nor will I commit to helping you without your parents' consent."

TEXAS EDUCATION AGENCY

Mr. Edwards at the Texas Education Agency thought the question was a bit novel. However, he could find no reason a student could not move from one grade by skipping another as long as they first satisfied the requirements of the grade in between. He found no law or rule governing the situation. He outlined the process and evidence necessary to make it work. The requirements were that the local district had to be convinced the student had passed each grade with the same quality of work that was required of every other student in that grade. The student had to show passing grades in four core subjects with a 70 percent or better average for each course in both the seventh and eighth grades. He stated further that a letter from the school principal listing and certifying the passing scores had to be sent to the receiving school and placed in the cumulative student file to act as evidence.

Asked how to document the passing scores for the Texas Education Agency, Mr. Edwards answered, "We will never get involved in this. Once you satisfy the local school district, the question is answered and you simply allow her to move forward."

LOCAL RESEARCH

The next conversation I had on this subject was with Superintendent Mr. Lehmann. I called him next. My relationship with Mr. Lehmann was very strained at this point. He was a new superintendent with an old set of assistant superintendents. He was in the process of removing all assistant superintendents, and he was not planning on doing this in a very nice way. I was one of those being removed. He accomplished this by temporarily eliminating the Curriculum and Instruction Department and moving all administrators elsewhere in the system or convincing them to retire. I was being moved to the position of principal at a low-performing middle school.

"Mr. Lehmann, this is Hillrey Dufner. I have a question for you as superintendent of schools."

His tone suggested that he did not want to be bothered, especially by me. "Dr. Dufner, I am very busy. What is your question?"

"We have a student in sixth grade who wants to move to ninth grade next fall. I have called TEA. They said the ultimate decision is ours. I have searched the local policies and found no rule and I know of no precedent—"

He did not allow me time to get to the question. "Dr. Dufner, this is your decision. If you can certify the student to move two grades, then do it. Just remember, if the student moves and is not successful, it will be on your head."

"Thank you, Mr. Lehmann. I will handle it." I did not see Mr. Lehmann as a superintendent who had students as his priority.

Another call seemed prudent. Mrs. Pullian was principal of Gaby's campus, after all.

"Mrs. Pullian, this is Dr. Dufner. Could you meet with me at nine thirty Friday morning?

"Let me check. Yes, sir, nine thirty will be fine. What is this about?"

"Just a minor matter really, Mrs. Pullian, I'm sure we can handle it together. Please meet me in my office."

BREAKTHROUGH

At the meeting that Friday, I revealed the results of my research to Mrs. Pullian, and outlined a tentative plan for Gaby to skip seventh and eighth grade. Mrs. Pullian objected to the plan on the grounds of missed social development. She expressed concern about two things. She was afraid that Gaby might be overly stressed if moved from dealing with twelve-year-olds to dealing and competing with fourteen- and fifteen-year-olds. She was also concerned that if this were allowed, the district would be inundated with requests from recent immigrants who had been placed two years below their peers to skip multiple grades. She said, "Dr. Dufner, as a professional, I have the right to withhold my recommendation for this child to move ahead two grades. I do not think it would be good for her, and I will not approve."

I had known Mrs. Pullian for over eight years. She was a risk-taker and innovator at heart, but would never place a child in a position to be hurt. She could be depended on to speak her mind, but as stubborn as she could be, she was open to having her mind changed if you could build a good enough case. "Mrs. Pullian, as a professional dedicated to meeting the needs of children, I cannot see how you can withhold your recommendation. This child is willing to work hard for what she wants. She just wants a chance. If she meets the criteria I have outlined, I will recommend the move. Legally, all you can do is approve her passing to the seventh grade; then her progress is no longer your responsibility, it's mine. We will not discuss this further, but I want your input. I may be on campus several times in these final seven weeks of school attending to this matter. Do you wish to be kept aware of our progress?"

She seemed to be relieved that she did not have to make the ultimate decision. "Yes, thank you, I do. I will be interested in whether she will commit to such a work load. If she says she will, I want to know if she actually follows through. By the way, I *will* register my objections with Mr. Lehmann."

"Mrs. Pullian, if you truly believe this is bad for Gabriela, I expect you to object. However, I also expect that this objection will stay between you, Mr. Lehmann, and me. Gabriela should not know anything of these negotiations."

"Of course, but you have already talked with him haven't you?"

"Yes, ma'am, I have. Mr. Lehmann placed the entire matter at my discretion, and I intend to see it through."

"Well, in that case, I will not object. I will do whatever I can to help you. Wouldn't it be exciting if she actually pulls it off?"

I was not prepared for such a sudden and decisive change of commitment from Mrs. Pullian. In past encounters, she had proven stalwart and determined, sometimes beyond my ability to see reason. She had won her share of academic squabbles with me in the days when we were equals on the ladder of hierarchy. One thing was in her favor; I never doubted her sincerity. She would fight hard when she felt she was in the right. Her giving in was not merely a sign of her acquiescing to the boss; she would not do that. Her principles would not allow her to give in to a decision she did not believe in. I understood that she gave in because she was beginning to doubt her stance was right. Now it was my task to involve her and get her pulling for the student. This was not a difficult job.

"Thank you, Mrs. Pullian. I could use your help on a couple of things. First, we may need your help establishing passing criteria. Will you help?"

"I have a couple of ideas that may be helpful," she answered with a little excitement in her voice. "I did some research too. For one thing, teaching writing to Gaby may not be necessary. She already writes very well, and I believe at or above the average ninth-grade level. Perhaps we could have her write a monitored essay and present it to the ninth grade teacher of gifted writers to see if she believes the essay would compete favorably with the other ninth graders. If it does, we can simply sign off that she has passed writing. But the essay must first be scored according to the state guidelines for eighth graders; meaning it has to meet the standards of composition, punctuation, and grammar."

"Thank you, Mrs. Pullian. I see you have been thinking about this little venture in positive terms as well. Will you take care of setting up the monitored essay? I will recruit the assistance of Mrs. White at the high school. I know her well, and she will pull no punches. She will give us an honest and accurate evaluation."

"Dr. Dufner, if this girl makes the attempt, I want her to succeed. I refused her request mainly because I had no way to offer her any assistance. I have been pushing you, because I wanted to know how much you could be depended on to help. Neither I nor my staff will be available to assist her this summer or to monitor her progress. Help for Gabriela will have to come from you or those you recruit. I needed to be sure you were willing to see this through. I am satisfied that you will not leave Gabriela to fail. Now, as for Mrs. White, perhaps you should simply ask whether the writing compares favorably to her students. Mrs. White tends to be a little snobbish and condescending about such things, so you will get a more complete evaluation if she thinks she is looking to have the student in her class. Why don't you submit the writing sample without Gaby's name attached? The less she knows about what we are up to, the better. She is an excellent choice to objectively evaluate the writing."

Grinning because of the vote of confidence I had just received from a professional I respected, I countered, "Actually, we are jumping a little ahead, Mrs. Pullian. Gabriela has not yet seen how much she will have to read and comprehend. After she knows how much is to be done, she must be committed to complete the work. I have to be convinced that she is serious, able, and has the support of her family. I am scheduled to meet with her on Monday in order to show her how much she will have to do to qualify to go to ninth grade from sixth. If she is not overwhelmed at the volume and agrees to do the work, we will work out a schedule with benchmarks so we can tell if she is on schedule to complete the work by mid-August. I have a good feeling about this."

Mrs. Pullian and I parted ways. She left my office and went about her business. I felt that both of us were rather excited by the prospect of this new venture that would definitely put us in the unfamiliar position of operating outside of normal school procedures.

THE SECOND MEETING WITH GABY

On Monday, April 6, 1993, I took three trips from my old Volkswagen Vanagon to the library in order to transport all the books and paperwork I had gathered to show Gabriela. I had spent several hours over the weekend gathering books and running copies of seventh and eighth grade curricula as well as the passing standards for both the seventh and eighth grades. Beginning on June 1, I was to take over as principal of Cuellar Middle School. I took on few new tasks at the executive director's office so I would leave few, if any, unfinished tasks.

When Gabriela entered the library for our appointment, she again looked nervously from side to side while walking toward the table I was leaning on. She seemed to be searching for possible witnesses to the conversation. I had the books and materials spread out over a large library table, seventh-grade materials on one end and eighth on the other.

"Good morning, Gabriela. Come on over."

"Good morning, Dr. Dufner." Gabriela was smiling nervously. A hint of apprehension raised the tenor of her voice. She was definitely nervous about my answer, but the materials on the table seemed to suggest something positive to her. She touched a couple of the books and glanced at the titles as she waited for me to speak.

"As you can see, I brought all the books you will need to work your way through if you want to move forward. I also brought the objectives and descriptions of all the courses you will have to pass in order to make it to ninth grade next year. This end is seventh grade," I said, indicating the end of the table away from her, "and that end, starting with that stack of books, is the eighth-grade. Do you think you will be able to complete all this by the start of school next year?" My expectation was that she would see the sheer volume of work and be somewhat daunted or at least consider what she was committing herself to. I expected her to withdraw or to lower her expectations to only skipping seventh grade instead of both seventh and eighth grade.

Gabriela did not answer the question directly, but her face brightened and her nervousness gave way to an air of expectation. She asked a question that assumed a positive response. "Can I start now?"

Unprepared for the question, I delayed and decided to test her commitment a little more. "You haven't yet made it through sixth grade. In addition, you have not shown me that your parents are behind you on this venture. I must have documentation for both before I can agree to the arrangement."

Gabriela grasped what I had said and read it correctly. "So, now it is your decision?" she asked. "Everyone else has agreed?"

"Yes, it is my decision whether to go ahead with this project or not. What did your parents say?"

Gabriela sat down at the table and slumped a little in her seat.

"My father will say no. I talked to my mother a little, and she is a little worried but will let me, but she cannot answer for my father." She looked at me, pleading in her eyes. "Would you come to my house and talk to my father? He would not say no to you. He would respect your position, and I think he would agree. You could convince him."

"I don't know. Gabriela, one of my requirements was that your parents agree. I expected you to get that agreement."

"I know and I wanted to, but you don't understand. If my father says no, and no one talks to him, that will be the end of it. He will never change his mind once he makes a decision, and with only me proposing it to him, he *will* say no. If *you* talk to him, he cannot say no. Well, at least it will be harder for him to say no to you than to me. You are a well-respected man, a boss in the school. He will listen to you. I am the only girl in my family. He will expect me to stay at home and care for my parents and help my brothers go to school and college. *I* want to graduate from high school, and *I* want to go to college. If I ask my father, I fear all my hopes for college will be decided at once. I must win one little battle at a time. Please, Dr. Dufner, come to my house and talk to my father." Tears welled in Gabriela's eyes and one ran down her cheek to drop from her chin to her chest, leaving a dark spot on her blue blouse. I thought that her intuition must have told her of my weakness when it comes to crying females.

Gabriela's plea was both logical and emotional. I was totally disarmed by the level of desire this girl had for education and achievement. I held great sympathy for anyone caught in a situation not of their own making that threatened to change their lives for the worse. I was also not so experienced that I was beyond being influenced by the tears of a young girl. Before I thought it through, I agreed to go to Gabriela's house to talk to her parents.

While waiting for the meeting with Gabriela's parents, I visited with each of Gabriela's teachers, asking whether they would agree to allow her to begin assignments from seventh-grade material, and I asked what that would do to her standing in sixth grade. Each and every one of them agreed to help her and a couple of other students begin the seventh-grade material. They even volunteered to grade the work the students completed. In addition, they acknowledged that Gabriela was the top student in each of her classes. Each teacher also said that if she did as well with the new material as she was in the current, she would not lose her standing in sixth grade. They decided that, even if she did nothing, Gaby would still pass to seventh grade with high honors. Once again, she was the top of her class.

13

Meeting With Gaby's Parents

THE NEIGHBORHOOD

I drove to the Garza house on the Friday evening following my meeting with Gabriela. My appointment was set for eight o'clock in the evening. Gaby said that by that time, Mr. Garza would have made it home, eaten supper, and showered. He would be settled for the night, and I would have his undivided attention. Over the phone, Gaby had given me directions and landmarks so that I could find her house in the dark. Her directions were meticulous and exact, giving me no option but to drive directly to the Garzas' front door.

Misgivings about my role in the conversation I was about to have ran through my mind as I drove through the most sparsely-populated area of Hidalgo County toward their house. Gaby would want me to be convincing, and I felt that I must be informative and encouraging. The decision had to be made by her parents. If I went in only trying to be convincing, the decision was mine. No matter how much I believed in it, the decision was not mine to make.

Gaby's neighborhood told a story of poverty. The poor conditions were revealed through small houses built of used and leftover materials, discarded vehicles sitting idly and rusting in yards, and gravel streets woefully in need of grading. However, the neighborhood did have the electricity, running water, and sewer services that were lacking in many *colonias* (literally 'colonies' Used to refer to outlying subdivisions populated by poor recent immigrants) along the Texas-Mexico border. I had visited many neighborhoods in greater need, so the state of housing in Gabriela's neighborhood did not surprise me. It was what it was. I had seen worse and had lived in much worse as a child.

The road was deeply rutted and had many potholes and erosion marks. The odor of burning garbage was heavy on the air. Loud and lively *Tejano* (Slang for a mix of Texas and Mexican) music from two different locations and two different radio stations drowned out most other noises in the colonia and identified the neighborhood as Hispanic.

As directed, I turned right at the neighborhood convenience store and began watching for the second street to the right. "XIII" was spray-painted in black over the mustard-colored east wall of the small convenience store just under a barred window. "XIII" indicated that members of the Mexican Mafia gang claimed the neighborhood. The symbol "C2," standing for "Cuellar Two," appeared in blue spray-paint below and to the right of the XIII. C2 was the only gang that remained to rival the XIIIs in this colonia. Latin Kings, Crips, Bloods, and a half-dozen other local gangs had all moved on. I briefly reviewed the history of the gang activity in the Weslaco-Mercedez area in my mind. In the preceding two years, two teenage boys had been killed, while four were wounded and several beaten severely in this general area as a result of gang violence. And those were only the cases reported. The actual toll was in all likelihood much higher. The XIIIs had gained an upper hand after some struggle. *What a waste*, I thought as I recalled Julian, another boy of fourteen who had been beaten to death with a baseball bat by a rival gang, and Antonio, a boy of fifteen in prison for the remainder of his life for the brutal murder of a rival gang member.

Throughout the trip to the Garza home, I questioned myself over and again about the purpose of my visit and the advisability of traveling into gang-infested neighborhoods after dark. My Volkswagen Vanagon still bore the marks of a permanent-marker tagging carried out by Latin Kings in another colonia to the north. I had made a home visit to a colonia served by Weslaco ISD. When I was ready to leave, I needed help getting the old bus started. A group of six youngsters volunteered. I later found out their real purpose. As some of the youngsters pushed to help me start the van, one busied himself marking gang signs on the back door of the vehicle. For a time, my van became a traveling advertisement for the LKs.

BUCKING TRADITIONS

Being somewhat familiar with Mexican culture, I knew a little about the traditional attitudes that Gaby feared would keep her from college. It was common for a child of the family, usually a girl, to be chosen to stay home and care for the parents instead of going to college, getting married, or pursuing a career. Gaby was the only girl in the family and had come to understand through Papi's conversations about the future that he wanted his boys to move on to higher education while she remained at home. I wondered about the advisability of using my influence to interrupt the application of this or any other cultural tradition. At the same time, I reasoned that Gabriela was certainly not a traditional sort of Mexican girl. She was as headstrong and determined as another girl I had helped buck another tradition several years before. My mind wandered back to my first year of teaching and the eleventh-grade girl who had asked for my help.

The tradition she helped turn over in a small community in East Texas, was the one that demanded unmarried pregnant girls leave school to have their children. Once sent away, they seldom returned to finish. In addition, once they were gone, if they returned, they were not welcomed back. In fact, efforts by schools were generally aimed at keeping girls with children out of school. Kay had accepted being sent away, but came back to school before her child was born. She was successful in completing her schooling with her class, but not without a fight with the principal, superintendent, and school board, and not without the persistent ridicule and persecution from classmates and a few of her teachers. I was not in a position of any particular power in that fight, but I did have the strength that comes from believing you are in the right. Kay had won and, although it had been threatened, I had not been dismissed.

Dreams. They make all the difference, I thought to myself. Dreams cause people to break with tradition. Kay had dreams that she could not give up.

By not giving up, she changed the culture and thinking of a community and its high school.

I wondered if Gabriela had dreams strong enough to carry her through this fight. She certainly had little trouble sucking me into the battle. I chuckled at myself for being so easily pulled into this discussion with Gaby's parents. I wondered who would be watching Gabriela to see if she would be successful. Other pregnant girls in Kay's community made it through school by following her example. Who else would succeed because Gabriela would not give up? *Maybe*, I thought with a shrug, shifting in the bucket seat. *Maybe it will be me.* I hadn't been very inspired lately. *Kay turned me into a teacher whose main concern was his students. What will helping Gabriela do for me? How will I grow from this struggle? Tonight's results, or at least the discussion, may be a measure of the struggle ahead."*

THE MEETING

A small black dog ran toward my front tire, barking and nipping ineffectively as I turned the Vanagon into the Garza driveway. The house was small. It looked like it could have four rooms. I sat for a moment, preparing myself to get out and begin this chapter of the adventure. *Maybe four rooms. And I think Gabriela said there were four children. How can poverty produce such a diversity of thinking?* To Julian, poverty had been an excuse to join a gang. A better dream had been the reason to leave it. Now he was dead. A sadness came over me as I thought of the very bright, funny, and engaging boy who had once had a great future but was now dead and buried, and whose death I had not come to grips with. *To Gabriela, this same poverty is a reason to dream big, focus, and struggle as hard as she must to get out of the poverty. Gabriela wants to be the proverbial butterfly. She wants to soar. She wants to have a meaningful life by her own definition*, I thought.

The small house was covered with slate siding that had been painted a shade of lime green sometime in the forgotten past. Trim around the door and windows had been painted white at about that same forgotten time. The house had been painted green and white long enough ago that bare wood showed in streaks through the peeling paint of the trim around the front door and window. The front door was slightly to the right of center in a front wall that supported a gable roof built symmetrically over the small house. A single bare bulb shined light into the yard from an uncovered fixture above the door.

The outside screen door sagged a little, as screen doors are want to do when they are subjected to the constant traffic of little children who can never decide whether to stay in or out. The panel of screen next to the door handle hung loosely, torn from the top outside corner. Few mosquitoes could miss the opening. The night was warm and swarmed with night insects, most of which had their own unique way of making people uncomfortable. In spite of the insects, the solid wooden door had been left open. It seemed insect bites were preferable to the oppressive heat of South Texas.

As I walked toward the house, I could see through the screen door and into a lighted kitchen/living room. An older version of Gabriela was cleaning the dining table and walking back and forth to the kitchen cabinets. The kitchen was dominated by a big black gas stove. Mrs. Garza was the only person in the house within my line of sight. The black dog that had chased my front tire, barked playfully at me and nipped at my feet. He grabbed the cuffs of my trousers in his teeth and pulled then released repeatedly as I walked to the door. I knocked gently on the faded white trim around the screen, rattling the door against the frame.

At the sound of my knocking, Mrs. Garza jerked her head around to face the door and walked quickly to open it. She unlatched the screen and welcomed me warmly. "*Bienvenido, señor. Pasele, entre, entre.* (Welcome, sir. Come in. Come in.)" She smiled warmly and turned to the side, motioning me into the room. Sanjuanita Garza showed me to a chair that had seen many better days but seemed to be the best chair in the kitchen. I sat down gingerly, not trusting the chair to withstand much in the way of weight. I did not know that the chair offered me had once belonged to Gaby's Abuelita Fela. It was part of a set that had passed on to her parents as a wedding gift. It was a great compliment to be offered one of those chairs, not because of the construction, but because of *who* had owned them. In Sanjuanita's mind, I think, it was the most honored place to sit in the house.

"*Gabriela, ven! Ya llego el señor. El maestro esta en la cocina. Ven!* (Gabriela, come! The sir has come. The teacher is in the kitchen. Come!)" Mrs. Garza's voice was gentle and coaxing even while the commands for Gabriela to come to the kitchen were emphatic. The kitchen was not large as far as kitchens go, but it seemed to be about a third of the small house. It was filled with the fading but still enticing odors of a meal completed but not yet forgotten. I read from Mrs. Garza's manner that she was very shy around strangers and that she was a very traditional Mexican wife, submissive to her husband. Her face was an older version of her daughter's and her eyes seemed to be evaluating me. There was also a hint of great intelligence, hard-earned wisdom, and great expectation showing in her dark eyes surrounded by tiny crow's-feet that radiated along both temples. She had a wisp of graying hair hanging loose that she pushed behind her ear but had fallen again.

Chairs sat empty along the wall beside the dining table, and a bench extended along the full length of the table on the kitchen side. The table was old sixties Formica scrubbed clean and shiny, still serviceable. To the left of the front door, as one entered from outside, a framed opening in the kitchen wall the size of a passage door was covered by a curtain made from yellow print material. Dishwater smelling of lemons still filled a large pan sitting on the cabinet. Open shelves, painted white and in the same disrepair as the outside trim of the house sat under the kitchen counter, extending along the right wall and holding a small array of cooking pots, skillets, dishes, and canned foodstuffs. Part of the open shelves had been curtained. An opening to another part of the house was directly in line with the front door and was covered by a maroon curtain. *Must be the master bedroom*, I thought absently. Just to the right of the maroon opening sat the black, gas, cook-stove, looming large, almost ominously, in the small room. The kitchen spoke of a large family, young children, a loving mother, and not much in the way of luxury. It spoke of poverty and a constant struggle to provide for the growing needs of growing children. In spite of the poverty, the kitchen was a warm, inviting, and comfortable place, even to someone unfamiliar with the family and a relative stranger to the culture.

Shortly, Gabriela appeared through the yellow curtain from the room to the left of the entry door. She was followed closely by a little brother she introduced as Casper. "I have told my parents that you have something to talk to them about. I also told them you do not speak much Spanish, so I will have to translate. *Mama, donde esta papa?*"

"*El es en el cuarto; se esta vistiendo.* (He is in the bedroom. He is dressing.)"

"Dr. Dufner, my father will be here soon. He has completed his shower and is getting himself dressed to meet you. Can I get you something to drink?"

Remembering my manners, and the dire straits this family seemed to be living in, I requested a glass of water. My 'manners' came from the frequent admonitions and instructions of Mrs. Irma Gonzalez, a long-time resident of the Rio Grande Valley, who said, "Never refuse hospitality from a poor family, but don't make demands they may have trouble fulfilling. If you ask for something they do not have, or cannot easily get, they will be ashamed. If you smell fresh coffee, accept a cup. If you see a pitcher of lemonade, accept a small glass, otherwise, ask for water." Gabriela left Casper sitting at the table and walked to the cabinet to get the water from a pitcher. Mrs. Garza took the dishpan through the maroon curtain, then reappeared shortly through the same curtain and wiped the pan dry with a dish towel. After placing the dishpan under the counter and hanging the towel from a nail to dry, and still drying her hands on her apron, Sanjuanita walked to the table and sat on the end of the bench farthest from me. She rested her arms on the table in front of her and sat silently looking from her children to me. She seemed to be waiting expectantly, but still studying me. From her body language, I gathered that Mrs. Garza was fully aware of the purpose of my visit and was fully in support of Gabriela, but that the decision was not hers to make. She would support her husband without question, as would any traditionally submissive Mexican wife.

Shortly after Sanjuanita sat down, Mr. Garza appeared through the maroon curtain buttoning the top two buttons on his shirt. Mr. Garza had a ruddy complexion with blue eyes, thick reddish-brown hair, a strong square jaw, and a perpetual smile showing even, white teeth and a seemingly benign nature.

"*Buenas tardes, señor! Bienvenido a me casa,*" he said as he looked into my eyes and shook my hand in sincere welcome. He was dressed in a casual white-and-red plaid, cotton shirt and clean, well-pressed khaki trousers. He seemed genuinely happy to see a stranger in his house. Throughout the conversation, he was a gracious, welcoming host.

"*Gracias, señor.*" (Thank you, sir) I knew a little Spanish but was reserved in my use of the language. I tried to avoid making a big mistake.

"*Papa, el señor Dr. Dufner es un maestro de escuela; es como un director como el Profesor Vargas.*" I did not know enough of Gaby's history at that time to be complimented by a favorable comparison to Profesor Vargas. She had not told me much of him or her great esteem for this humble and dedicated teacher.

"*Sí, claro es un hombre muy importante.*"

Gaby spoke to me. "I just told my father that you are one of the bosses at my school and a teacher. He said, 'Clearly you are a man of great importance.'" I smiled at being called a boss. I did not think of myself in those terms. Even my secretary was discouraged from using that title toward me.

Mr. Garza seemed to be impressed that a man with the title of doctor and who was a boss in a large school district would visit his house. Then for a few moments, he seemed to become suspicious that the meeting might not be on a subject of his liking. His eyes narrowed as he studied the "director de la escuela" carefully, but he retained his good spirit and welcoming attitude as the conversation, as is traditional in the Mexican culture, skirted the primary reason for the visit until something of a relationship could be developed.

Gabriela translated almost every word of the conversation as it went back and forth. As is customary in Mexican cultures, before getting to business, Mr. Garza and I passed pleasantries and talked about the Garza and Dufner children, the weather, farming sugar cane, how quickly the Rio Grande Valley was filling up with people, how difficult it had become to "cross the border" for a simple visit, and a sundry of other topics. None of these things had anything to do with the visit but everything to do with establishing lines of communication and finding common ground for a friendship.

At the appropriate time, Mr. Garza's face grew serious. *"Bueno,"* he began as he asked about the reason for the visit. I began explaining my mission. I talked about Gabriela's excellent grades and study habits, and the fact that Gabriela was placed in fifth grade in Weslaco when she had passed to seventh grade in Mexico, as well as about her retention in fifth grade even though she had made excellent grades. Mr. Garza nodded, indicating that he knew these statements to be true, but he did not speak for a while. After spending considerable time building up the background for Gaby's request, I asked what Mr. Garza would think about Gabriela moving up to a higher grade since she was able and of the right age. At first Mr. Garza seemed to be concerned. Then he asked if that meant she would be out of school sooner. "Yes," I assured him. "In fact if she is able to complete the work she has agreed to, she will graduate with her class at the age of eighteen instead of twenty-one, and be ready for college."

Mr. Garza seemed to ignore the reference to college and instead asked how much this endeavor would cost him. I was glad to be able to answer with certainty. "Nothing. Gabriela will do the work, and a teacher of the relevant subject she is studying or I will grade the work. If she does well, she will be able to move up through seventh and eighth grade this summer."

"What about how much she will miss?"

I had to be honest and direct. "No doubt she will miss some things, and some things she will not learn as well as she might if she had more time. However, she seems to learn things better than most who work much longer than she does. Her goal seems to be to complete enough of the course of study to begin in the ninth grade this fall. I believe she can do this if she works hard at it, and I believe she will be committed enough to complete both grades. And," I added, "if she only completes one grade this summer, she will still be ahead of where she is now."

Gabriela nodded and translated, adding some of her own embellishments and a plea for his permission. *"Por favor, Papi! Por favor!"*

"Pues..." (Well...) Mr. Garza nodded and then said in Spanish, "She is a stubborn girl when she wants something badly."

I responded, "Stubborn is what you call someone who wants something from you that you don't want to give because of the cost or because it is bad for them. Determined is what you call someone who will not give up on a dream. Gabriela is determined. If you and your wife give your permission, she can begin immediately and have a little more time than just the summer." I had turned into a salesman after all. It did not bother me.

Mr. Garza acknowledged the difference then asked directly, "What do you get out of this? Why are you interested in my daughter passing two grades in the summer?" The question was a right-angle turn in the conversation and not one I expected, but not one for which I was unprepared.

"It has been a long time since I have helped a child fulfill a dream. When I first started teaching, education was only a job to support my family. Now, I can do nothing else because of children like Gabriela who challenge me to make the school system work for them. What do I get out of this? I do not get money, *nunca dinero*. My pay will not change if she completes the courses or not. Some of my professional status will be lost if she does not. There is some risk to my career. I stand to lose some things. However, while I am not sure how, I am certain that something good will come of this; something that will help me grow. I think I will be a better person and learn something that will help me be better able to help the next child who challenges me."

THE DECISION

Mr. Garza had been rocking back in his chair, tempting fate to send him over backward. At this point, he rocked forward and put his chair down on its four legs. The discussion was over. He seemed satisfied with what he had heard. Mr. Garza sat upright in his chair, locked his hands behind his head, and then leaned forward on the table with his elbows, looking into a distance that wasn't there. Clearly he was pleased that his daughter was so well thought of, and he was close to a decision. He looked long and hard at his wife, as if to ask her opinion. She shrugged and opened her hands palms up just above the table, as if to say, "It's your decision." That movement told me that she was in complete agreement. Had she objected, Mr. Garza would have all he needed to refuse his permission. Gabriela sat very still, seeming to hold her breath. Casper crawled into her lap, seeming to realize that his Gabriela was stressed and needed support.

"*Bueno*. It's Okay," Mr. **Garza** answered in both Spanish and English. He continued in Spanish, saying that it was a good plan. He admonished Gabriela to work hard and complete the curriculum. "Don't start it if you are not going to complete it."

Gabriela exhaled loudly as if she had been holding her breath all this time, and began talking rapidly, promising faithfully to work hard and complete the project. The business satisfactorily completed, for the next half-hour Mr. Garza and I talked of other things and laughed often as Gabriela happily translated. In that short time, I developed a genuine liking for the man and a healthy respect for his willingness to work hard to accomplish his goals. It was clear to me that Gabriela had inherited the best from each of her parents. Her gentle nature and determination came from her mother, while her willingness to work hard and challenge the system came from her father. Finally I excused myself and left for home. Before leaving, I had to promise to visit again. In front of her father, Gabriela thanked me for my help and promised again to be faithful in getting the work done. She then walked me to my van with Casper safely in tow and thanked me again with a wide grin spread across her face. "I have already started the reading," she announced as I ignited the engine of the old van.

14

Getting Started

FIRST CREDIT

On Monday morning, I called Mrs. Pullian to provide an essay prompt and ask her to give Gabriela one hour to write as we had agreed. She was to be sure Gaby had no assistance from other students or reference materials such as a dictionary or thesaurus. After receiving her assurances, I promised to go by the school that afternoon to pick up the essay for grading. I also asked Mrs. Pullian to ask the librarian to help Gabriela check out all the seventh and eighth grade textbooks I had brought to her campus. Later in the day, Mrs. Pullian called to let me know that the essay was written and the books were officially checked out to Gabriela, but they would be stored in the library. Gaby told Mrs. Pullian that she had no safe place to keep that many books at her house, so Mrs. Pullian provided a place in the library to store the books she was not using.

She could leave them there until she needed them, but she would have to take them with her at the end of the school year.

At my urging, Mrs. White took the essay and agreed to score it based on ninth grade standards. Two days later, she called me to let me know she felt the paper would be B work in her ninth grade honors class. Given that information, Mrs. Pullian and I agreed that while Gabriela would have several writing assignments for other courses, she had now gained our certification for language arts writing credit in both the seventh and eighth grade. She had proven she had the vocabulary and writing skills necessary to survive in high school. Mrs. Pullian was given the privilege of informing Gabriela that she now had accomplished two credits toward her goal.

LOGISTICS FOR THE SUMMER

Beginning the first day of June, I was to take over as principal of Cuellar Middle School. Cuellar was the same seventh and eighth grade campus Gabriela was assigned to attend in the fall. The school had been rated as "low performing" by the State Education Agency, and the superintendent wanted changes made that would positively impact student scores. I was chosen to lead the effort. I had no illusions. I knew I was not chosen because the Superintendent wanted the school improved, but because he assumed I would fail like the previous four principals had. If I failed, he could get rid of me without much trouble. I could only quit or do my best.

During the week before school let out for the summer, I went to Mary Hoge, Gaby's sixth-grade campus, to check on her progress and complete a study plan for the summer.

Gaby met me in the library and we briefly discussed her seventh-grade coursework, which seemed to be going well. I gave her a writing assignment on Texas' fight for independence. Before leaving, I mentioned that there was an empty office in the administrative building of the Cuellar campus that she could use during workdays throughout the summer. The office had a large table she could employ to spread out her work, and she could have access to assistance from teachers and me when she needed it. The arrangement would also make testing and keeping up with her progress much easier.

Gaby brightened at the suggestion. "That sounds good. I would like that. I was worried about where I would keep all these books and papers at my house. But there is a problem."

"Okay, what is that?"

"I do not have transportation to get to Cuellar every day. We have only one pickup, and Papi needs it for work. Could you come get me in the mornings?"

I thought for a moment before making a decision and answered, "Yes. Yes, I can. We will begin the Monday after school is dismissed. You will need to bring a lunch. There is no food service at Cuellar this summer. And also, I like to get to work early. I will need to pick you up at about six-thirty in the morning so I can be on campus by seven, and I normally leave school around five in the afternoon."

"Then I will get up early and pack a lunch. Thank you. I will see you early Monday morning."

"Okay, but we must take care of these books. You do not have a way to take them home and bring them to Cuellar. Let's pack all that you don't need immediately and load them in to my vehicle. I will take them to Cuellar for you. They will be in your office by Monday."

Gabriela smiled at the mention of her own office but said nothing about it. She helped pack the books in boxes provided by the librarian and helped load them into my Vanagon before returning to class.

THE SUMMER BEGINS; HELP ARRIVES

At six-thirty on Monday morning, May 26, 1992, Gabriela was waiting with her books and her lunch when I pulled the old brown Vanagon into her driveway. She quickly said her good-byes to her mother and Casper, then climbed into the front passenger seat of my van. She was on her way to work on her self-imposed project. At the office, she quickly got down to business, and the day went by quickly. She worked through some Texas history, stopping to ask questions about vocabulary and terminology she did not understand.

Late that morning, Mrs. Sturgis came by to visit with me. Mrs. Sturgis and I had worked together on a couple of innovative district projects and had been friends for several years, but we had never worked together closely on a campus. I had recruited her for the Cuellar campus, and she had requested a transfer to teach social studies to eighth-graders. Since there was an opening, I quickly approved the transfer and showed her to her classroom. After the business of moving her from one campus to another was complete, I gave her a sideways glance and asked, "Do you want to get involved in something exciting?"

"I knew there was a reason you were being so helpful," she said with an expectant smile. "What do you have up your sleeve now?" she asked with a grin and more than a little suspicion in her voice. I told her about Gabriela and the plan she had to move through two grades in one three-month period. Then, before enlisting her help, I introduced her to Gaby. When we returned to my office, she said, "That is a precious child, and so very smart. What do you need me to do?"

"Well, I thought I might be able to handle all her testing and tutoring, but I'm quickly getting in over my head. I am well versed in mathematics and science, but frankly I'm not as in tune with the social studies requirements for seventh and eighth grade as you are. In addition, the workload to get this campus ready for opening school this fall is tremendous. I don't have the time to read ahead of Gaby to be prepared for her questions as well as write a final exam. If you are willing, I would like you to construct or help me construct a final exam for both seventh grade Texas history and eighth grade American History. They need to be comprehensive enough to prove whether she has learned the basic concepts outlined by the Texas Education Agency's Essential Elements. I need to be able to prove she has passed the courses by TEA standards. Keep in mind that I have no budget. I can't pay you a thing. All I can offer is the chance to assist a very determined girl in realizing her dream."

"You could not pay me to help her. There is no amount of money that I would take. But if it is alright with you, I would like to come to campus a couple of days and use my room to help her through some of the rougher concepts, then I could do the testing. The testing will probably take two days, one for each course. Like I said, money will not suffice as payment, but for a chance like this, for a student like her… isn't it the dream of every real teacher? Isn't this what we got into the business for? I definitely want to be part of this." Ms. Sturgis was almost giggling. "Oh, I *will* exact payment in the form of some time spent helping me get my room in order, but that *she* will pay."

"Well then, dear lady, you shall be part of this little venture. Let's go talk to Gaby about the details."

At around five that afternoon, I called it a day and took Gabriela home. And so it went for the rest of the week. Gaby had already gotten a head start on both history courses, and by the end of the week she had completed both social studies courses under the guidance of Mrs. Sturgis. Through April and that first week of summer, Gaby had managed to read both books, write three papers per course, finish numerous chapter tests, and pass both final exams. She made a ninety-six percent in Texas history and a seventy-five percent in American history. Mrs. Sturgis certified her passing grades for credit. I was very pleased that Gabriela was ahead of her schedule, but she knew that algebra loomed on the near horizon. That eighth-grade math course alone would take more time than two courses in any other subject. Gabriela was disappointed in the seventy-five percent in American History and spoke of doing the course over, but ultimately she decided the grade would have to do since there were many more courses to complete and so little time. She seemed pleased with her progress when I delivered her home that Friday, May 30, 1993. When she said her cheerful good-bye and walked gaily to her front door, she had no clue that she would soon endure the greatest ordeal of her young life. I had no idea that was the last I would see her for a long time.

Everyone has trying times. Everyone has pain, sadness, and frustration to overcome. The pain each of us has to endure seems to be tailored to us, to our strengths and weakness. These become our tests of will, both of body and spirit. Some people become victims and lie down under the new weight. A few face them head-on and never give up. Any new pain inflicted on these few stalwart people becomes a source of inspiration. They use the trial to become more and endure more; they use it to become stronger and to overcome the current hardship and those to come. In so doing, they learn to live their dreams. Such is life. Some not so stalwart souls claim victim status and choose to be trampled underfoot, while a few become stronger and soar while turning the trial into a source of strength. On the morning of May 31, 1993, Gaby was unknowingly on the brink of a great trial that would test her strength of body and spirit, as well as her resolve to achieve her goal.

15

Tragedy

TO THE STORE FOR RIBBON

The last day of May was a bright, sunny, beautiful, but swelteringly-hot day. It also began as a happy day at the Garza house. There was to be a graduation. Close friends of the family were celebrating two graduations that afternoon; both a young man and a young lady from the family had graduated from high school. Now there was to be a fiesta to celebrate the milestone. Mrs. Garza had sewn a brown dress with white polka-dots for Gaby to wear to the party. Finished, pressed, and ready to wear, it hung suspended on a hanger from a nail in the wall beside the front door of the Garza house. Gaby was very proud of the dress and could not wait to be seen in it.

The crowded house was busy with preparations. There was food to cook, clothing to be cleaned and pressed, baths to be taken, and presents to be wrapped. One of Gaby's uncles had decided to go fishing at the coast instead of attending the party, but his wife, Gaby's tia Rosi, wanted to go, and decided to come to the Garzas' house to help with the preparations, but since she did not drive, she would have to be picked up in Weslaco. The ladies at the Garza house soon realized that they were short on ribbon for the presents and arranged a trip to the store in Mercedez to buy ribbon and a few other odds and ends. In the same trip, they would pick up Gaby's aunt.

Tio Juan, Rosi's husband was on his way to the Texas coast. He had planned to spend the entire weekend fishing with his friends. He offered Gaby's dad his vehicle, a green Ford Bronco that was in top shape. Beto's pickup was very small, but the Bronco was large enough to drive Gaby's parents, Tia Rosi, and the kids to the graduation party if they squeezed in tightly. Gaby's father accepted the offer and asked Sanjuanita and Gaby to get ready to go into town in order to pick up the little Bronco, Tia Rosi, and the ribbon. The family received company immediately before leaving. Relatives from Sanjuanita's side of the family had decided to stop by; Gaby's Tia Cristina and her Prima Frances arrived to pitch in with the preparations. The new arrivals had no problem staying behind while the family went to town; they were happy to take care of Gaby's brother, Gamaliel, while awaiting the family's return.

Gaby dressed in khaki shorts and a pink blouse printed with the brown silhouettes of South American Indians playing music on wind instruments and dancing around her torso. She also wore leather sandals that Papi had just bought for her a week before. She had braided her hair and took a small coin purse for her personal purchases. When all were ready, everyone squeezed into the little truck. Gaby sat on the center console and Casper kneeled behind her while Sanjuanita sat in the passenger seat. They looked forward to traveling in Tio Juan's Bronco with more room.

The drive to Tia Rosi's house took about fifteen minutes; she lived in Weslaco in the old downtown area. Tia Rosi was anxiously and happily waiting for them. She gave keys to the Bronco to Beto. Tia Rosi talked excitedly as she prepared to go with the Garza family. They all got in the Bronco and started for the store. Beto drove, Sanjuanita was on the passenger side, Gaby was in the back seat behind her dad, and Tia Rosi was sitting in the back seat behind Sanjuanita. Casper and Gaby's five-year-old primo, Raul, were sitting in the open area behind the back seat where a tool box had been installed; there was no third row seat for them. ThUS arranged they went to HEB, a Texas chain grocery store in Weslaco, to get the ribbon. Gaby remembers that someone picked out one blue bow and one pink bow.

THE INTERSECTION

The happy group traveled along Texas Blvd, heading north from Weslaco toward Mile Eleven where they would turn east toward the Garza house. Tia Rosi was almost giddy as she carried on a light conversation while joking about going out without her husband. Like Sanjuanita, Tia Rosi was a traditional Mexican woman whose eyes were only for her husband, but she enjoyed a good laugh. She had decided to go with them to the graduation party, because she was left alone with her small son. Her husband was going fishing and her oldest daughter had gone up north to work in the fields; the daughter had left that same Saturday early in the morning. Her middle son had left with Tio Juan to go fishing, and she was left at home with the youngest son, Raul, who was only five years old. She joked about her plans to dance with another man and tell Tio Juan all about it. The mood was light, and they were certainly having a good time.

When they turned right on Mile Eleven North going east, they had no idea what awaited them. Gaby was not paying attention to the road. Absently she listened to Tia Rosi's chatter. They had traveled the road many times before, and there was nothing new to see. There was a four-way stop prior to an isolated ranch followed by miles of fields until the next paved cross-road, FM 1015.

At the same time the happy family was traveling east, a drunk driver was traveling very fast northward in a heavy van on Mile Four East. The ditches at the intersection of Mile Eleven North and Mile Four East were overgrown with weeds and tall Johnson grass. Visibility at the intersection was very limited from any direction. Visibility was especially limited from the south, the direction from which the speeding van was coming, and from the east, the direction from which the Garza family traveled.

As the green Bronco entered the intersection, Mr. Garza glanced up to see the other vehicle speeding toward them from the south, but no one else saw the van speeding toward them. There was no time for Beto to do more than scream, *"Everyone hold on!"* before a violent, rending, and grinding impact slammed the Bronco. For Gaby, everything went black instantly. She did not see the car approach, and she was unconscious so suddenly that she did not feel the impact. She has never regained memory of the accident.

Gaby's father was able to hold on to the steering wheel, but no one else had time to react to his warning, nor was there anything really to hold onto. The van was driving north-bound on the caliche road when it hit the Bronco on the right side, directly into the front passenger's seat. Sanjuanita and Tia Rosi were crushed inside the Bronco before it began to flip. After hitting the Bronco, the van careened into a vertical concrete irrigation valve standpipe that stood about twelve feet tall. The concrete held, and the van was stopped instantly.

The green Bronco with the Garza family inside came apart at the seam in the roof. The back part of the roof, which was made of plastic, flew off immediately, landing a hundred yards down the Mile Four and Half North road, north of the intersection. Because the roof came off, the four people in the back of the Bronco were exposed. The rest of the car flipped seven times and landed on its driver's side nearly a quarter-mile north of the intersection, scattering people in its wake. Mr. Garza was the only one left in the Bronco when it finally skidded to a stop lying on the driver's side with all four wheels in the air. Mr. Garza had held on to the steering wheel, and he had been the only one in the vehicle wearing a seatbelt.

Confused, dizzy, and in pain from being slammed around the cabin of the Bronco, Mr. Garza asked if anyone else was in the car. No one answered. He looked around and found no one, so he unbuckled his seatbelt and climbed up and out through the front passenger's window, and began looking for the rest of the family. In the distance, he could see that the offending van had careened off the road to the right and into a standpipe. The driver of the van was dead on impact, but that man was not Beto's concern. He did not approach the other vehicle at first.

The driver's side tires of the truck were suspended slightly above the pavement, and the Bronco rocked unsteadily as the front wheels continued to turn on their axels. Mr. Garza was disoriented and hurting from the violent thrashing his body had taken. He knew he had to do something to save the rest of the family and that he needed help, but there was no one around. The road where the accident occurred had little traffic and was surrounded mostly by fields. Adding to the problem, weeds and Johnson grass had grown unchecked that spring so that the accident and its aftermath was largely hidden from view unless you happened to be on the road or at the intersection.

SEARCHING FOR THE FAMILY

The first member of his family that Mr. Garza spotted was Tia Rosi, his sister-in-law. She was lying very still in the middle of the pavement not far from the overturned Bronco. As he walked toward her, he thought he could tell from her position and lack of movement that she was dead, but of course he could not know for sure. He immediately went to her, hoping to find her awake. She was not; she was limp. Tia Rosi had taken the brunt of the impact. She had been directly in the path of the speeding van and closest to the right side of the car. Gilberto knew how to check her pulse, so he did. She was dead; he was certain. Never before had he been in an accident where one of his passengers died. He began going into shock and was unable to move for a few seconds as the seriousness of the situation became clear. He said a small prayer for Tia Rosi and asked for forgiveness for having killed her. He knew he had to move on and search for the rest of the family, so he moved her body to the side of the road and began searching.

Next, Beto spied Sanjuanita lying on the west side of the pavement further up the road toward the intersection. She was lying almost still, but she was crying in pain from the broken bones in her shoulder. Her face and clothing were covered with blood. He could hardly believe it was his wife. Her broken collar bone was sticking out of her skin and her entire upper-right side had been crushed. Beto could see that her shoulder was broken. She was conscious and able to tell him that she was fine. She sprayed blood as she talked, begging Gilberto to look for little Casper and Gaby. Gilberto thanked God for allowing him to find Sanjuanita alive. Thanking God was something he was not used to doing. Beto took most things for granted, be they good or bad. He had never experienced anything this horrible. Silently he begged God for another person to show up to help him. Daylight was beginning to fade. The accident occurred close to six in the evening.

As gently as he could, Beto dragged Sanjuanita close to Tia Rosi's body. With tears running down his face and fighting shock, he moved on to search for the rest of the family. Suddenly, he heard a youngster crying and quickly followed the sound, searching through the tall weeds and grass growing in the ditch. It was Raul, Gaby's five-year-old cousin. The little boy was awake and seemed to have no injuries at all. He seemed to have no broken bones or bruises; all he had was a cat-scratch on his right cheek. Mr. Garza didn't have time to explain anything and after carrying the boy to his mother's body, told him sternly to sit next to his mom. Raul sat calmly and began to caress his mother, looking for some comfort from her. The little boy did not understand that his mother was no longer able to respond to him.

Time was going by quickly, and Beto still had to find little Casper and his only daughter. Though growing weak from shock and in great pain, he was still able to think. He figured that Casper would have to be close to Raul since they had been sitting next to each other in the back seat. He looked through the thick growth of tall grass and weeds again. He first found Casper's shoe but saw no sign of Casper. At the sight he lost control and began screaming. He screamed for help and begged God to help him through this difficult time. Beto got on his hands and knees to search for Casper. He was desperately fighting through the tall grass, shoving it down and out of his way in clumps until he finally spotted Casper's body, lying still, hidden by tall weeds in the ditch. Casper's face was clean; there was no blood and no cuts. Beto took this as a good sign and Beto felt a sense of great relief. But then he thought of Tia Rosi; she was clean too, and there was nothing broken that he could see, but she had died. Beto quickly picked Casper up, held him close, and began to feel him, making sure he was breathing. Casper was breathing, but did not respond to being picked up or to his name being called. It was as if he was asleep and could not wake up. Beto saw that there was blood matting his hair. Looking more closely, he could see a deep cut in Casper's scalp. Casper was breathing steadily, but still did not respond to his father's voice or touch. Gilberto carried the boy to the street and placed him next to his mother. He asked her to take care of him while he looked for Gaby. He had now found everyone but his little girl.

Mr. Garza searched again in both directions and on both sides of the road, still hoping for someone to drive by, for someone to call an ambulance, but there was no one to be seen. He kept screaming for help and screaming Gaby's name, but he heard nothing in response. He searched both sides of the road again, but was unable to find her in the ditches. On an impulse, he went to check on the driver of the van. The man was still strapped in the vehicle by his seatbelt, but he looked dead. Beto checked the man's neck for a pulse and, since he found none, felt it was best to leave him inside the vehicle. There was nothing to be gained and only time lost if he paid attention to the dead man.

Satisfied there was nothing he could do for the man in the van, Beto began again searching for his girl. Every once in a while, he would go back to check on the family members he had found. He continued this routine for what seemed like hours to him. After a final search of the ditches, after too many times to count, he went again to check on Sanjuanita and the two children. Gaby's mother was still awake, saying words Gilberto could not understand. Blood was still flowing from her mouth, and her front teeth were gone. What he knew she must be saying was that he still had to find Gaby. He checked Tia Rosi's pulse again, hoping that he had been wrong, but she still showed no signs of being alive. She wasn't. Raul was awake and next to his mom, stroking her hair and begging her to wake up. Beto moved on to Casper and held him tightly for a few moments. Placing his ear on the boy's chest, he could hear a light heartbeat and knew Casper was still alive, and he was hopeful for him. Beto had to look for Gaby. He hadn't heard her crying, nor had he seen anything of hers that might lead him to her. He felt he had looked everywhere and was growing more desperate with each place he searched.

HELP ARRIVES

Again Beto screamed for help. He prayed for God to send him someone to help find his girl and help him get everyone to a doctor. Having spent that excess emotional energy, he was calmer now; he stopped screaming and looked around, realizing that the closest ranch house was about half a mile away. Planning to go to the ranch house he could see, Beto was instructing Raul not to move when he heard someone ask, "Do you need help?" At first he thought it was his imagination, but when he turned around, he felt that God had answered his prayers.

A man on horseback had ridden up quietly. His horse was standing close behind Beto. When he saw help had arrived, Beto began screaming his name to the man, screaming the story of the wreck and finding his family, and screaming that he could not find his girl. Sensing that Beto was going into shock, the man stepped down from his horse and began to dial his phone while trying to calm him. After reporting the accident and giving directions to the 911 operator, he turned off the phone and began to talk to Beto in an attempt to keep him from going into shock. To keep Beto calm, he told Beto that he knew who he was because he had gone fishing with

Beto's brother. Beto asked the man to stay with Rosi, Sanjuanita, Raul, and Casper while he went to look for Gaby.

Beto went back to the truck again to double check whether she had remained inside the Bronco. He didn't find her inside. He walked around the truck and spied one of her shoes close by. He picked it up and moved faster toward the field, but she was nowhere in sight. Tormented by the accident he felt he had caused and the fact that Gaby was still missing, he started walking back toward the pile of bodies he had gathered. It was then that he saw her foot, right next to the rear truck tire that was suspended above the pavement. Her body lay directly under the rear wheel that was still suspended in the air. The truck was gently rocking back and forth in the slight breeze, as if it was trying to decide which way to fall. If the truck fell on its wheels, the tire would have fallen on top of Gaby and crushed any life she may have had left right out of her. Mr. Garza quickly pulled Gaby away from the truck and checked to see if she was breathing. He felt nothing. He felt for her pulse and on feeling none began to scream and cry and pray. He carried her as he had when she was a baby, crying and repeating the same question over and over; *"Por qué? Por qué? (Why? Why?)"*

He placed Gaby next to Sanjuanita and told her he needed to go get help. The man told him help was on the way, and that he needed to just sit down and rest. Beto knelt next to Gaby to say a prayer so she could rest in peace. While he was praying, her body was hit by a light breeze, moving her hair and lifting her blouse. He moved to cover her stomach, and when he did so, he saw her stomach move up and down. She was breathing! She was not dead! Beto checked her pulse and cradled her in his lap, rocking back and forth while he began thanking God for her life.

The man who had so miraculously ridden up to help stood close by, not knowing what else he could do to help. He watched silently as Beto went back and forth from crying his sorrow and remorse for killing someone, to whispering his thanks to God for sparing those who lived. The man wondered at the dichotomous response life and death could arouse in people. Darkness was quickly closing the day. The man did not interfere, seeming to know that while Beto cared for the family, he would not be likely to go into shock himself.

EMERGENCY CREWS ARRIVE

A few minutes later an ambulance arrived. The EMS crew quickly began triage, separating the victims according to the seriousness of their injuries and prescribing emergency treatments. Shortly thereafter, a Life Flight Helicopter stirred up a cloud of dust as it landed on the street, and the county coroner arrived. The helicopter had been called to deliver Gabriela to Valley Baptist Hospital in Harlingen. She was the most seriously hurt and in grave danger from a severe head trauma. German (Casper) was taken by ambulance to a hospital in McAllen.

Shortly after the EMS crew arrived, the sun finished its job of setting, leaving the emergency workers in the twilight. They could not see to do their jobs without lights. Soon there were police cars, ambulances, and a helicopter, all lending their lights to the rescue efforts. The road was completely blocked by vehicles, and by that time a group of curiosity seekers had gathered around the perimeter. Two officers were kept busy just to keep them at a distance. The man who had dialed the emergency number had also called Gaby's uncle, so news of the accident was soon spreading in all directions. Young Gilberto, Gaby's older brother, got the news while at home with his other aunt, cousin, and Gamaliel. Not much detail was given to him when he called other than that his family had been involved in an accident and it was serious.

He grabbed his aunt's car keys and drove quickly to the accident site. When he arrived and saw bodies lying on the unpaved street, he panicked. He asked the authorities to let him through and told them that it was his family lying on the street. He didn't see his father anywhere, but he saw his mother covered in blood. He saw Casper and Gaby lying, seemingly lifeless, on the hard-packed street. He begged the authorities to let him get closer, but they held him back. He had to be forcibly restrained from going to them. He repeatedly screamed, "That's my family! That's my family!" but he was not allowed to get close enough to tell how seriously any of them were hurt. No one could tell him who was alive and who was not. Everyone except Gabriela and German were taken to Knapp Hospital in Weslaco. Beto Jr. waited at the scene until everyone had been routed to the hospital. He saw that Tia Rosi was taken to a funeral home in Weslaco.

CONTINUING LIFE AND PAIN

That night was very difficult for Mr. Garza. It was very emotionally numbing and difficult to confirm Tia Rosi's death for the coroner, know that his kids were in hospitals in different cities, and have his wife so badly injured. He knew he had driven the Bronco into harm's way, and it weighed heavily on his heart. He felt the pain of blame over the death and injuries. It was early Sunday morning before he was finally able to go home. For a long while, after all was taken care of, he still was not able to rest.

The next day, Sunday, June 1, no one remembered it was young Beto's birthday. The events were so overwhelming that even the birthday boy himself forgot about it. The day was spent figuring out the logistics of who was going to see whom in what hospital, who was going to cook which meals, and so on. Sanjuanita was allowed to go home on Sunday afternoon. Her injuries did not require that she be treated at the hospital. Her lips had been cut badly and she had lost most of her front teeth, but there was nothing more the hospital could do for her. Mrs. Garza was wrapped as well as the doctors could to help her broken scapula and collar bone heal. Her shoulder blade eventually healed, but the broken ends were not well matched, and they grew together crooked. At the hospital, all they could do for her was stop the bleeding, stitch the cuts, and bind her wounds. After her shoulder blade was relocated, she didn't need to stay at the hospital. Raul was allowed to go home; he had no injuries or apparent physical trauma.

German was sent to a hospital in McAllen. He had a cut in his scalp which required seven stitches, and he had fallen into a deep coma. After awaking, German had a long and difficult recovery. He was in the coma for seven days. The doctors said he had some brain damage, and he had no memory of how to speak. He had to learn to talk again. After awakening, because he hadn't suffered any other injuries, he was allowed to go home. German's continuing problem was that he could not move his tongue. His parents were content at the time to hear that he could go home. His mom figured that once he got to the house, he would begin talking. She thought that maybe he was afraid to speak because of the strange environment in the hospital and had refused to respond to doctors and nurses out of fear. Her thoughts were wrong. Casper did not speak for a long time, not even when he was given his favorite toy. On Sunday June 15. Gaby's parents attended mass at the San Juan Shrine. Sanjuanita prayed hard for her injured children. When mass was over, she asked Casper if there was anything he wanted. He responded with, "Mi juguete." (my toy). Sanjuanita's brief celebration, though heartfelt and in praise of God's mercy, was muted by her continuing pain and sadness over Rosi's death and Gaby's injuries. Gaby was continually on her mind, but she was comforted that German would recover.

Gaby had been sent to Valley Baptist Hospital in Harlingen. She was in a deep coma from which the doctors held little hope she would awaken. For the first week after the accident, Gaby's parents had to travel to both Harlengen and McAllen on a daily basis to visit their children. Other family members were drafted to sit with the each injured child while the parents were resting or with the other child.

Tia Rosi's daughter flew home from Minnesota on a private plane to attend her mother's funeral service. The Garzas' life had forever changed. Beto's duties now consisted of taking care of the house and Gamaliel. He also had to continue working to provide money for the household expenses. Gamaliel and Beto Jr. had to learn to do a lot of Sanjuanita's work, such as laundry and washing dishes. Tia Cristina and Cousin Frances volunteered to frequently cook for the family and occasionally sit with Gaby in the hospital. The house was very busy, especially in the afternoon, with constant visitors and volunteers. Three days after the accident, the family buried Tia Rosi. A week later, Gabriela remained in a coma.

16

In the Hospital

PULLING THE PLUG

During the helicopter flight to the hospital, through the initial physical examination, and for many days afterward, Gaby remained in a coma. For the next week, relatives took turns sitting with her in the hospital when Sanjuanita or Beto could not be there. If Gaby should wake up while her parents were gone, they wanted people she knew to be at her side. Even relatives Gaby didn't see very often volunteered to help take care of her. When Gaby first woke up from the coma, her Cousin Frances was sitting next to the bed. She immediately called the nurse and Gaby's parents. Gaby sat up and began saying things Francis couldn't understand. It sounded as if she were speaking in another language, carrying on a conversation with someone other than Frances, someone not in the room. When the nurse came in and tried to get her to lie down, Gaby began fighting with the nurse, physically resisting lying down, and demanding to go home. Her only memory of that brief awakening is that there was a lot of blood, and she was scared. All she could think was that she wanted to go home to her mother. It seemed to her that there was a lot of blood, and the nurses would not tell her from what injury the blood came, or what had happened. It is not clear if there actually was blood that Gaby saw, or if it was in her imagination.

The doctor came in and requested that the cousin leave the room. By the time Gaby's parents made it to the hospital room, she had fallen back into a deep coma. She did not respond to Beto or Sanjuanita, or the doctor's probing. The doctor explained that Gaby had experienced a seizure, sort of like a 'brain attack.' The doctor also stated that he did not believe she would ever completely wake up.

After the seizure, Gaby was transferred to another room full of machines that monitored every bodily function that could be measured by technology. She was there until June 19. During the days before June nineteenth, her parents visited her on a daily basis. During their visits, they would bring her gifts that people had brought for her, mostly stuffed animals. Their visit on June nineteenth had been scheduled. The doctor had requested that they visit her at a certain time. All her immediate family over the age of eighteen was allowed in the room. When her parents arrived with her older brother, Beto, the doctor informed them that all machines that were supporting her had to be disconnected. They explained that it had been too many days since she had awakened, and she was not responding. They said that brain-wave tests indicated that she was dead, and the only reason she was breathing was that the machine was forcing her lungs to fill with air and release carbon dioxide. Her parents and brother were devastated by the news. The doctor left the room for a few minutes, telling them he'd be back with the proper staff to take care of the procedure. He told them they should say their good-byes. The room was filled with weeping, sadness, and fearful dread as the family began to realize what was very soon ahead of them. Family members touched Gaby in various ways as they spoke to her, hoping for some sign that she would wake up and recover.

Doctors had watched the deteriorating situation resulting from Gabriela's injuries. Blood clots had formed in her brain. She was comatose and completely paralyzed on her right side. The clots were life-threatening, and because medication had not been effective in dissolving them, they would have to be broken up using surgical procedures, but the doctors all agreed that Gaby was not strong enough to survive the surgery. Not wishing to make a premature decision, they waited for some sign of brain activity. After several more days of watching and evaluating, they reached a critical point and the decision was made to call the family into her room to say their final good-byes before all life support was removed.

THE AWAKENING

After the doctor left to inform the proper staff and give the orders, the family gathered around her bed and tearfully said their good-byes. The doctor in charge brought one colleague and a few nurses back with him. The team began disconnecting machines one by one until Gaby's body was free of wires and tubes. Last of all, as each member of the family expressed great sadness, they removed the breathing tube from her throat. Shortly, they could no longer hear a heartbeat, and her breathing was becoming more and more shallow. Medically, any doctor would conclude that Gaby was dying and soon to be gone. Gaby's older brother held on to her legs and began screaming, "Wake up, Gaby! If you will come back, I will no longer fight with you. I love you, and I miss you. You need to wake up; you have to wake up! Please, wake up!" The doctors tried to get him off of her, but he held on to her legs and would not be moved.

Expecting Gabriela to fade quietly into eternity, the doctors, nurses, and family were utterly shocked when Gabriela's eyes fluttered then opened wide. Still expecting her to die, Mr. and Mrs. Garza held their collective breath. It took a few moments for those watching to realize that she was actually awake and breathing! Gabriela opened her eyes, looked around briefly, and then focused on her brother at her feet. "Why are you crying? Stop crying! I'm not going anywhere." She looked into the doctors' faces, thinking that they looked terrified. In a matter of a few seconds, all the wires and tubes connecting the many life-sustaining machines were plugged back in, all except the breathing machine; it was no longer needed. The doctor asked Gaby to continue talking and stay awake. The family began weeping, this time from joy, but there remained a sense of dread that the awakening was temporary.

Gaby had heard her brother's tearful requests that she stay and not go away. In a soft, calm, but firm voice, Gabriela assured him she was not going away, that she was going to be okay. Soon the Garza family was talking, making joyful noises, and welcoming her back. Shortly the nurses were back, shooing everyone except Mr. Garza out and offering to get Gabriela food.

It had been nearly three weeks since Gaby had eaten anything. She had instead been fed through tubes in her arms. Gaby's father was asked to stay with her so he could encourage her to chat, stay awake, and eat. When she was asked if she wanted to eat, she asked for a cup of Jell-O. Gaby talked with her Papi about going to the flea market to get a radio and some music to listen to. She stayed awake for a long time. Finally, the doctors felt it was safe for her to sleep. She ate little, only a spoonful or two of the red Jell-O, then went back to sleep. This time her sleep was a peaceful and restful sleep.

GABY'S REQUEST

There were a number of tests and doctor visits between naps, but those didn't bother Gaby. She was so confused that she had not yet realized she was in a hospital. After a long chat with her dad, she asked for her little brothers, Gamaliel and Casper. She was told they were home, and she could not see them until she got out of the hospital. It was then that she became fully aware that she was not at home. She suddenly realized that something really bad had happened, and no one had told her about it. She asked the nurse if she could see her brothers. Because the nurse could not help her, she asked the nurse to call in a doctor.

The doctor walked into the room and gave her a stern look. "What do you need? Wasn't the nurse here with you?"

The doctor had no clue how strong was Gaby's will and ability to be straightforward. Her response was something like, "Didn't she tell you? I want to see my little brothers, both of them, and I want to see them now!"

The doctor placed his hand on her right foot and said, "They are under-age and not allowed to come to your room."

Not at all satisfied with his answer, she replied, "Well, if they can't come, can I go see them?"

The doctor exhaled loudly and told her, "You can't go home just yet; you'll get to see them sometime soon." Gaby grew angry with his refusals and chided him,

"Why do you have to make this so difficult? If they can't come to the room, and I can't go home, can we visit in the waiting room, maybe? How about if I just see them from a window? Don't be so mean. Let me see my brothers. If you don't, I will start screaming."

Mr. Garza, who was still in the room, did not speak English, and therefore had little idea of what was being said. However, he understood from experience the kind of conversation Gabriela was having. He was very surprised when the doctor said to him, "I need you and your wife to come in tomorrow at eight in the morning. Bring someone that is fluent in English and Spanish. Also, when you come, bring your kids." Understanding both English and Spanish, Gaby had followed the conversation and was excited that she had won the argument. She was satisfied that she was going to see her brothers. It wasn't until the doctor left that she realized with some degree of fear and wonder that when the doctor had grabbed her right foot, she had not felt his hand. She was not yet aware that she was paralyzed on the right side of her body.

It seems now that Gaby, at least subconsciously, knew she was in a fight. Fighting with the doctors put a face on an enemy that was otherwise invisible. It was clear that, as exasperating as it was, the hospital staff knew Gaby had to respond in anger and frustration toward someone, and she needed her family too much to target them. The health-care people were doomed to fall at the point of her spear.

SURGERY

Early the next morning, when her parents and Tio Juan came to see her, the nurses transferred Gabriela to another bed. Gabriela noticed that, unlike her other bed, this one was on big rollers and very narrow. They gave her no explanation, only informing her of what had to be done to move her. She could see through a window that her mother and uncle were in the next room discussing something with a doctor. She could see her mother shaking her head and crying; then a little later, her uncle seemed to be signing papers. It was the morning of June twenty second.

Gaby was wheeled out of the hospital room still in the narrow bed. She was placed beside a window where she could finally see her brothers on the other side. They were playing on the grass outside. They could not see her, but she had at least seen them and was somewhat satisfied. After a few minutes, she was taken on the narrow bed with the big wheels to another part of the hospital. Traveling quietly and quickly through a fog, and between the stripes of bright ceiling lights, she saw her parents faces go by.

They both had tears running down their cheeks. She saw Tio Juan looking very sad. Suddenly the bed stopped moving. There were noises all around her but she could not make them out, nor could she see the people moving. Someone said something about smelling bubble gum, then she felt a mask being placed over her nose and mouth. She felt like she was suffocating. Suddenly there was no air. She fought back kicking and throwing punches, but very quickly the gas flowing through her mask won her over her efforts and she slept. Hours that seemed like minutes went by before she awoke strapped down to a bed in a strange room. He mother sat anxiously beside her.

No one had explained it to her, so Gaby was unaware that she had had blood clots in her brain from the trauma of the accident. Three weeks after the accident, blood clots remained that had not dissolved with medication. Since they did not dissolve, they had to be removed surgically. Her mother had been unable to sign the waiver for surgery after being told the chances for survival. The doctor explained that the surgery would have to invade her brain to remove the clots. He had also explained that, because of the location of the clots and her weakened condition, there was about an eighty percent chance that the probes would poke holes in blood vessels and Gaby would experience bleeding in her brain. There was a great chance that she would die during the surgery, or at the very least never be able to walk or talk again. But the doctors explained that the clots would certainly kill her, or turn her into a vegetable, if they were not removed. "At the very least," he explained, "the clots will cause her to have constant seizures, which are very dangerous in and of themselves."

The doctor explained that the procedure would take about an hour and be painless to Gaby. With Sanjuanita's permission, Tio Juan signed for her to have the surgery. Gabriela remembered later that the anesthetist had told her that the gas coming through the mask he put over her face would smell like bubble gum, but she also remembers thinking while she was fighting off the mask that she was suffocating, and that the man was a liar; the gas did not smell at all.

THE CHILDREN'S WARD

After a few hours in the recovery room, Gaby was transferred to the intensive care unit. She was not dying or in danger, but following such serious surgery, the doctors wanted to monitor her progress very closely.

The next day, Gaby was recovering well enough to be transferred to a room in the children's ward. In the room next to hers, through a glass window, she could see a number of bald children. Gaby was just getting settled into the room when about five kids were allowed to visit her. Many of the children she saw in that part of the hospital were there for cancer treatments. Most had thinning hair or were already bald because of the chemotherapy or radiation therapy to which they were being exposed. Among the children, Gabriela was one of the tallest, and she was the only one with a luxuriant head of long, dark hair. The other children visited her often. The little girls especially loved playing with her hair. They combed and plaited it, then took it down again and started all over, over and over again. Gabriela sat patiently, held up by straps, and allowed them to handle her hair as they wished.

Gaby stayed in that room for two days. She was assigned one particular nurse each shift to take care of her needs. Gabriela's daytime nurse was a young man from Brazil. He was tall and thin, and he had a distinctive Spanish accent. During her time in his care, he was very kind to her. He asked Gaby many questions, including what her favorite things were. Gaby responded to all of his questions without any concern or consideration for his intentions. She did not see this particular nurse as an enemy.

Perceiving that Gaby was bored, the young man asked her if she wanted anything while she was recovering in the room. She asked for a jigsaw puzzle to put together. He went away for a while then returned, bringing her a worn puzzle that originally had perhaps fifty pieces. Gaby had it together in a very short time, minus the missing pieces, and then asked for one that was more difficult. He brought her another puzzle from the children's ward that had a hundred pieces except for two that were missing. She put this one together in a short time as well and asked for a puzzle that would be a challenge. The young man could not find another one in the children's ward, so he left the hospital during a break and bought her a puzzle with five hundred pieces. She was temporarily satisfied with the challenge, although the new puzzle did not take her very long. She concentrated hard and worked intensely on the new puzzle until it was complete.

Gaby had not yet realized that she had no use of her right hand and leg. She was paralyzed on her right side, but she was not yet aware enough to notice that she was doing everything with her left hand. In her trauma and drug-induced confusion, she also had not realized that as of yet she had not attempted to walk, and she was being held in a sitting position by straps.

Later, the young nurse brought her a number of jigsaw puzzles and some posters of Michael Jordan. Somehow he got ahold of VHS tapes showcasing some of Jordan's most exciting basketball games. He put a lot of effort into making her stay in that room as pleasant as he could. He even drove to Pizza Hut to get her food, because she refused to eat hospital food. His kindness and attempts to please her stopped her for a time from complaining and asking to go home.

I WANT TO GO HOME!

After a few days when she was stable and out of danger, Gaby was moved from the children's ward to a double-occupancy hospital room. Almost immediately, she began to be eaten up with homesickness again. She slept for a while then called for a nurse. The hospital was very busy, so getting the attention of a nurse took time. When the nurse finally came to check on her, Gaby asked her the question she always asked, "When is the doctor coming? I want to go home."

"You can't go home. You can't even walk," the nurse responded. Gaby finally heard this statement but she had still not noticed that her right side was limp and non-responsive. The statement seemed so ridiculous that she dismissed it without exploring.

"I need to see the doctor so he can sign the papers for me to go home!"

"The doctor will make his rounds this afternoon. You can see him then, but you won't be going home for a long time. You have to learn to walk again."

The nurse's reference to her not being able to walk still did not register in Gaby's mind as a reality. She had not felt or considered that she might have any permanent damage from the injuries to her body. During the whole day, Gaby tried to stay awake so she would not be asleep when the doctor visited her on his rounds. Throughout the day, she would occasionally doze off then awaken with a start, hoping the doctor had not come and gone but wondering if he had. Several times that day, she called the nurse to find out whether the doctor had already made his rounds and when he was coming. She ate a little lunch, but she ate in a hurry to make sure she would be able to talk when he arrived. She also wanted to be ready to leave immediately. When the doctor finally came to her room on his rounds late that afternoon, Gaby was awake and very relieved to see him; but she still steeled herself for the argument she knew was to come. While he was looking over her chart, and before he could speak, she demanded that he allow her to go home.

"No, you can't go home. You just got out of brain surgery. For God's sake, girl, you can't even walk!"

"Yes, I can."

"You are paralyzed over half your body. You have no use of your right hand and no control over your right leg. The part of your brain that controls your right side is damaged. You will be in the hospital for a long time so we can get you into physical therapy and teach you to walk and use your arm. You need to be able do things for yourself instead of depending on others to do simple things for you."

"I want to go home now. I can do everything for myself."

The doctor's eyes shifted around the room, searching for a way to explain to the girl how much trouble she was in. An idea came to him and his eyes lit up as he spoke. "When you can walk to that bathroom," he said, pointing in the direction of a door Gaby could see but had not noticed before, "and back to your bed without help, then you can go home."

"When I can walk from here to the bathroom and back without help, I can go home?"

"Yes. Now we must talk about a plan for your recovery, including lots of physical therapy. Where are your parents?"

"They will be here to take me home. Can you call them and tell them to bring my clothes?"

The doctor gave up the argument and left the room after a cursory check of her vitals, bandages, and chart. He was still shaking his head in disbelief as he walked through the door into the hallway. Gaby surveyed her leg and her arm, suddenly realizing there was some truth to the claim that she was paralyzed. But, she dismissed the new information thinking that being paralyzed was an obstacle to overcome, not a reason to give up on going home. She decided she would meet the doctor's requirements by morning. She began planning for a night of learning to walk to the bathroom and back without help. *I should be able to do that in one night*, she thought as immediately she began struggling to get out of bed.

17

Disappeared

NO ONE HOME

On the morning of June second, the Monday after Gaby's wreck, I drove up to the Garza house to pick up Gabriela for work. I parked my brown van in front of the house as I had done the week before, expecting to see Gaby waiting at the front door. Things were very different from my expectations. On this cool, pleasant morning, I could sense that something was very different and very wrong. The house seemed abandoned. Not even the black dog greeted me to nip at the cuff of my trousers. The van was alone in the driveway and, with the motor off, everything was quiet. The delicious odor of *barbacoa* (A pungent and spicy dish usually made from the meat stripped from the head of a hog, and used as filling in breakfast tacos) wafted on the air. I stepped down from the van and walked to the door. There was no answer to my knock, so I knocked again, louder. Again there was no answer. There was no sound from the house, no light on, and no indication of human habitation. I did not detect even the usual leftover odor of a recently-cooked meal. The barbacoa odor came from a neighboring kitchen. There were many car tracks, in the fine dust of the driveway, but no one was home.

It was not unusual for people in this part of Texas, even whole families, to disappear suddenly, especially if recently emigrated from Mexico. However, I had never experienced a family's disappearance without any trace of explanation. It did not make sense. I could not bring myself to believe that Mr. Garza, or any of the family, were involved with drugs or any other illegal activity that might cause such a quick decision to leave. Nothing I could think of explained Gabriela's disappearance. I knew, or at least I thought I knew, the family was in the United States legally. But maybe that answered the question of why the family was gone; *Maybe they aren't legal.* Then I recalled that Mr. Garza worked at the sugar plant. The managers at that plant were very careful to hire only documented workers.

A very slight morning breeze blew steadily from the east as I waited for a few minutes, expecting something to happen that would reveal the answer to the mystery of their disappearance. Nothing happened. The house remained quiet. Puzzled and at a loss to explain the disappearance, I stood scratching my head for a few moments, then left the neighborhood, still wondering what could have happened.

Throughout the day, I continued to wonder what had happened to Gabriela and her family as I worked on the business of conducting summer school, scheduling students, hiring teachers, trimming the budget, and attending to the myriad of other concerns pertaining to opening school in the fall. I considered a roundup by the Immigration and Naturalization Service, or a maybe death in the family, or perhaps some windfall job had been offered to Mr. Garza at a distant location, but I could not imagine Mr. Garza making a sudden decision to return to Mexico. I gave up speculating and continued my day as a new principal taking on what was promising to be a difficult campus. Several times during the day and the days following, I called the Garzas' home telephone number. There was no answer. Twice that day I made the trip to the house with the same result. Later, I realized that my visits to the house coincided with the family's visits to the hospitals and Tia Rosi's funeral. I simply had made my calls and visits at the exact times no one would be home.

That week went by with no word from the Garza household, no news story on the TV, and no obituary notices that attracted my attention to explain the missing family. Looking back, I realize that Tia Rosi's obituary did appear, but it escaped my notice. I was looking for Gilberto or Gaby. Once again that week, at the appointed time, I drove to the little green-with-white-trim Garza house and its single outside light bulb, now dark. There was no sign of anyone having been at the house except for fresh car tracks in the driveway. I thought I knew that Gabriela would contact me eventually to let me know what had happened. I could not believe she would give up her quest, and certainly not without talking about it. It would appear unseemly to Gaby to leave or quit without explanation. Contacting me would be a matter of decorum.

Another week passed with no word. The telephone went unanswered. Wednesday of the second week, I knocked on the doors of several surrounding houses to inquire about the Garza family. Their neighbors seemed to know nothing of the Garza mystery, or they were not talking. I got the impression that I looked too official in my principal's uniform and too Anglo to get any answers in a neighborhood that almost certainly held individuals and perhaps entire families who were illegally in the United States.

MYSTERY SOLVED

On Friday of the second week, Gaby's older brother, Gilberto, came to my house. He was seeking assistance for his girlfriend who needed my help answering confusing questions about documents that were necessary to gain entrance into college in the fall. As I began working on the paperwork, I asked him about Gaby and the family.

"Oh, you don't know? Gaby is in the hospital. They had a car accident."

"How is she? How bad is it? Is she going to be released soon?"

"No, she is in a coma. She got hit in the head. My aunt died, and my mother has a broken shoulder. They don't know if Gaby is gonna make it."

"What hospital?"

"Valley Baptist in Harlingen."

"Can she have visitors?"

"Well…yeah, but she don't know nobody."

HOSPITAL VISIT

A few minutes later, I was on my way to the hospital dressed in a light-blue suit and red tie. Later, I could not recall why I had changed into my Sunday best, but it turned out to be a good move. Volunteers at the lobby's information desk gave me Gaby's room number and directions then warned me to check in at the nurses' station. The nurses on duty paid little attention to me as I approached the room and looked in.

There was a young girl lying on her back on the hospital bed, seemingly asleep. She had a bandage on her head, and her face was swollen almost beyond recognition. I assumed it was Gaby, but there seemed little resemblance to the lively, smiling girl I remembered. She had a tube taped to her mouth and many wires and tubes attached to her that ran to machines and monitors which fanned out on both sides of the bed, creating a symphony of quiet beeps and buzzes. A bag containing yellow liquid hung from the bottom rail of the bed, which indicated that a catheter was in use. An IV pole held two bags of clear liquid that were draining into her arm. A heart monitor beeped constantly, and what appeared to be a breathing machine wheezed regularly. The girl moaned audibly and moved slightly, but she did not seem to be aware of anything. A small woman, who I took to be Mrs. Garza, sat in a hospital chair with her head bowed. The chair was on a line between the door and the bed, directly facing the girl's head. I entered the room and stood quietly behind the woman in the chair. She was whispering a prayer as she manipulated rosary beads in her hands. The words were very quietly spoken and in Spanish, so there was little I could hear or understand. She did not seem to notice my presence. I stood for a moment taking in the scene before quietly retreating with a feeling of powerlessness in the face of immense, faceless opposition.

Feeling like an intruder at this very private and serious scene, and now fearful about the seriousness of Gabriela's injuries, I backed out of the room and walked to the nurses' desk. None of the three nurses at the station looked up as I approached. "Excuse me," I began. "Which of you is the nurse of record for Gabriela Garza?" All three nurses looked up, obviously concerned, and one stood.

"I'm Gabriela's nurse. What can I do for you?"

"Would you brief me on her condition and prognosis, please? I was made aware that she was in your care less than an hour ago."

"Well...." The nurse paused, somewhat confused. She wanted to answer, but was prevented from doing so. Her name tag read Raquel Maldonado. "We are allowed to give information only to her family; are you family?"

"I'm sorry. I am Dr. Dufner from Weslaco. I have been working with Gabriela for a little over two months." I reached out to shake hands while holding Nurse Maldonado's eyes with mine. After shaking her hand, I placed my hands in the side pockets of my dress coat in much the same manner as I had seen used by medical doctors. Then I continued without a pause. "Nurse Maldonado, I don't need specifics, only an update and prognosis. I can visit with her doctor later for details." Inside both pockets of my jacket my fingers were crossed, hoping the nurse would buy the ruse.

"Well, doctor, she has a severe head trauma with some clotting and has been in a coma since she was admitted." Then in an almost whisper, "Her condition seems to be getting worse, and her doctor doesn't think she is going to make it."

"Is her family here?"

"Yes, a member of her family sits in the room with her almost around the clock. They don't say much. Usually whoever is here with her just sits and prays and watches."

If anyone had asked me to swear that the girl in the bed was Gaby, I could not have. Wondering if I could have made a mistake in finding the room and intruded on a stranger, I asked if the room on the corner was Gaby's.

"No, she is in the second room on the left." I had been to the right room. The girl that was unconscious and hooked up to all those wires was Gaby.

"Thank you, Ms. Maldonado, you have been most helpful. I'll just step in for a moment." Reluctant to leave, yet not qualified to add to Gaby's treatment and not wanting to intrude, I went into the room quietly, standing for a moment five feet behind the woman in the chair. For a moment, I felt much like was in a funeral parlor looking into an open casket. Unable to shake the feeling, I left soundlessly as a lump grew in my throat.

The trip home was difficult. Tears kept welling up to cloud my vision. I kept thinking that there had to be something I could do to help, yet I knew that there was nothing. I had no power to fight this tragedy and no way to help Gaby heal. Visions of my visit to the Garza home and of Mrs. Garza, Beto, and Casper, all crowded into my mind alongside the recollection of

Gaby, lying there helplessly and terribly injured and swollen. I was wishing that I had said something. Except for Nurse Maldonado, no one would even know I had been there. I was just a visitor. I kept repeating to myself, *Just a visitor. Nothing to do. No one to notify. No way to help. Impotent in the face of powers of life and death.* By the time I got home, I had reached the same conclusion as the lady in the chair. Prayer seemed the only way to fight the demons of death. I prayed often over the next few days for Gaby's life to be spared and for her to be able to fulfill her dreams.

DISAPPEARED AGAIN

Having no way to receive updates except by visiting, I went back to the hospital twice more. Two days after the first visit, Sunday afternoon, I found the same scene and got the same result as the first visit. Nurse Maldonado recognized me and gave an update without being asked. The prognosis was not good.

Tuesday, four days after the first visit, was quite different. I went straight to Gaby's room only to find that a different patient's name was on the door. Gaby was gone! Questions flooded into my mind, and it felt like a hand was around my throat, choking the life from me. In a panic, I looked for Nurse Maldonado.

Nurse Maldonado was not on duty. Nurse Garcia, whom I had not seen before, did not seem to know anything about Gaby and had no record at the station of her having been there. All she seemed to know was that Gaby had been moved. Volunteers in the lobby did not have Gaby's name on their register except at the old room. I went quickly to the gift shop to buy a paper. Gaby's name was not in the obituaries. Back home, I called the Garza telephone number again. No answer. No answer for the next two days. I stopped calling but continued to check the newspaper. No record. I went home without an answer. No answers came for a few more weeks.

I later found out that at least part of the family was staying at home at night, but there was so much to do during the day that they got early starts in the morning. There were multiple visits to hospitals, several doctors with whom to make connections, a funeral to plan and attend, all in addition to work and chores. I had simply timed my visits and calls badly. With seemingly no way to find out about Gaby, I settled into my work routine and waited for word to come to me.

18

Going Home

QUALIFYING

Taking the doctor at his word, Gaby began immediately to work on the problem of getting to the bathroom and back to the bed without assistance. From the time of the accident until that evening, Gaby had not gone anywhere without someone helping or rolling her on a bed or in a wheelchair. Now, for the first time, she was shocked by the full realization that she had no use of her right leg and arm. She was paralyzed on the right side of her body. The doctor had been right about that. She put the shock aside, there was no time for self-pity, and she did not think about anything except getting to the bathroom. Her total singular focus was aimed toward walking to the bathroom. Neither her right hand and arm, nor foot and leg, would cooperate. As much as she willed them to do so, neither would move. She had to learn to walk even though she could not move her right leg or trust it to support her, and her right hand and arm could not grab or pull. In fact, instead of being a help to her, her arm and leg were in the way. They just hung limply.

Gaby maneuvered her body using her left hand and foot and pushed with her head. She managed to slip off the bed and unsteadily onto her feet. When she finally stood and supported her own weight, she was dizzy; her left leg was weak, her right was useless, and her body felt very heavy. Until that moment, alone at the side of her bed, she had not stood since before the accident, nearly four weeks past. Gaby decided that her left side had to take the lead. Her right leg and arm remained useless and heavy. For now she knew that her left leg had to support her weight. She continued trying to will her right leg into doing its part and her right hand into grabbing something to help. Neither would perform. Sweating with effort, dizzy, and trembling from exertion, she began a struggle that would last most of the night. On her first attempt at taking a step, all she did was fall to the floor then pull herself back to the bed and onto her feet again.

After that fall, she realized she was not alone in the room. There was an elderly woman in the other bed who expressed her displeasure at being awakened. Throughout the night, Gaby tried to keep from making noises that would awaken her. However, many times during the night her neighbor in the next bed fussed at Gaby for disturbing her rest. "Go to bed, and stop waking me up!" she complained.

Gaby used her left hand and leg to pull herself back upright facing the bed. She then turned around, pivoting on her left foot. Thinking and planning first, she took a trembling step of only a couple of inches with her left leg, leaning on whatever she could grasp with her left hand. She then dragged her right leg until it was even with her left. Then she tried to repeat the action. During the second try for a short step, her left leg buckled and again she fell. Throughout the night, over and over with only brief rests to gather her strength, Gaby took a step, fell, struggled back to the bed and began again. Two steps, three steps, fall, get back up, rest, try again, and fall again. Many times during that night she fell attempting to get to the bathroom. Occasionally, she lay down to get a brief rest. Luck was with her, because the nurse's visits were timed perfectly. They caught her resting between attempts instead of lying on the floor struggling to get up.

Gaby found, after several failed attempts, that her right leg would hold some weight if she stood so her knee was locked. When she progressed about two feet into the open space with nothing to lean on, she focused on her balance and staying upright while attempting to make progress. When her left leg began trembling so badly that she thought it would buckle, she turned back to the bed, falling in it to rest up for the next attempt. She felt better. The attempt had not been a complete success, but it was well-defined progress. She did not end up on the floor. Activity seemed to clear her head and the stretching of her muscles after so long a rest gave them renewed power.

Throughout the night, she pulled herself up, turned, took a step, fell, and dragged herself back to the bed repeatedly in seemingly futile attempts to walk to the bathroom and back. Finally, almost at the end of her strength and just before dawn, she succeeded in approximating a walk to the bathroom, then turned back to face her hospital bed and struggled to it without assistance. Sweating, trembling, and exhausted from the effort, but glowing with the satisfaction and excitement that she now qualified to go home, she dragged herself into the bed and rested, awaiting the doctor's visit. Gaby was extremely tired, but she felt very good. She had accomplished something very difficult. She was exhilarated, and for the first time in as long as she could remember, she was hungry.

FACING THE DOCTOR

Gaby ate her breakfast with great gusto, but now fully aware of the limitations of her right hand. Immediately after breakfast, she allowed herself a much-needed nap. She knew the doctor would not be by any time soon.

After she awakened from her nap refreshed and satisfied, she began her vigil to make sure the doctor did not come through without talking to her. Throughout the day Gaby rested, but also tried to stay awake so she could talk to the doctor. Very much like the day before, she occasionally dozed off and awoke with a start, wondering if she had missed him. And like the day before, several times she asked her roommate and the nurses who came through whether the doctor had been to the room. He had not yet made a visit. When it was served, she ate her lunch sparingly and quickly, always watchful for the white coat and stethoscope.

The doctor arrived in the middle of that afternoon. While he looked at her charts, and before he could ask any question, again Gaby demanded he sign the papers to allow her to go home.

"We already talked about this. You can't go home. You are paralyzed on your right side. You can't walk yet. We have a lot of therapy to do."

"You said when I walked to the bathroom and back to bed by myself, I could go home."

"Well, yes, when you can walk by yourself, you will be ready to go home."

"Then I am ready. I walked to the bathroom and back to bed last night. I worked all night to do it, but I did it by myself. Now you have to let me go home."

The argument went back and forth for a good while with the doctor insisting she must stay in the hospital because she had just undergone very serious surgery and it was not safe for her to be at home. Gaby countered his every argument by insisting that she had walked and that there were plenty of people in her family to take care of her; it was perfectly safe for her to be at home. She assured him she would be better monitored at home than in the hospital, because someone would be with her all the time instead of only every two hours. Finally, the doctor had exhausted his battery of reasons and caved in the face of her unrelenting stubbornness. "I have never seen anyone with such a strong desire to go home. Maybe it will be the best thing for you." He signed the release and walked out, shaking his head and muttering to himself. Gaby wasted no time gloating over her victory. She began making preparations immediately.

FINALLY, GOING HOME

Shortly after the doctor left the room, Gaby's nurse came to help her prepare to go home. No one had been able to contact them, so when Gaby's parents arrived with two of the boys, they were prepared for only a visit and totally unprepared to take her home. They had no clothes for her and had come in Mr. Garza's small, red, single-cab pickup. There was no place to lay her down for the trip home except in the bed of the truck. Mr. Garza offered to go home and get her some clothes and borrow a vehicle more suited to her needs, but Gaby would not hear of him leaving without her. Beto Garza was not up to an argument with his strong-minded daughter that he knew he would lose, so with a slight shrug of resignation, the issue was settled and he began planning how he would get her home in the cramped quarters of the pickup.

Gaby was wearing the typical hospital gown that opened in the back. That was as close to clothing as the hospital would provide. Modesty was a concern, along with expediency, so Gaby requested they wrap her in a sheet before sitting her in the wheelchair for delivery to the truck. A very sympathetic nurse brought them a sheet she said was ready for disposal anyway. So they wrapped Gaby as she had requested. Mr. Garza went to get the truck in position to receive her while the nurse pushed Gaby's chair to the exit.

It was an ordinary day for the middle of summer in the Rio Grande Valley of Texas: bright, hot, and muggy. However, to Gaby, there had never been such a beautiful day. It had been weeks since she had been out of a hospital room. She immediately began noticing greenery, marveling at the fresh air, listening to birds chirp, and gazing at the deep blueness of the sky, cherishing all the natural things she had been deprived of in the hospital for so long. She was seeing trees, grass, and sky as if for the first time, and they were beautiful. Although she did not feel well yet, it felt good to be out of the confines of the hospital, and she was happy that she was going home to finish her recovery.

There was little room for another passenger in the truck, especially one in Gaby's condition, so the boys had to ride in the back in the open air. Like most boys, they preferred the back anyway. Mrs. Garza got herself in position as best she could while still nursing a sore shoulder, and Mr. Garza came from behind the steering wheel to help. Beto picked Gaby up, cradling her like a baby, like he had after he found her at the site of the accident. He gently placed her in her mother's lap for the ride home. Beto noticed for the first time how much weight Gaby had lost. She was too easy to pick up. Gaby was comforted by being held in her mother's arms the whole way home. She already felt very much better just being away from the hospital and with her family. *Now*, she thought, *I can get well.* She was very tired and sleepy just from being placed in the truck, but she was very happy to be back in the care of her family.

19

At Home

TOO MANY VISITORS

When they arrived home, Mr. Garza lifted Gaby out of her mother's lap and easily *too easily*, he thought, carried her inside the house. Hurried preparations were made to put clean sheets on her parents' bed and do what little else they could to make her comfortable. Mrs. Garza began almost immediately preparing food. Exhausted from the ordeal of coming home, Gaby rested and slept. When she awoke, an often repeated cycle of family and well-wishers visited with her, often wanting to know what they could do to help.

From the bed, Gaby could converse with her family and the occasional friends who gathered around her. They were full of questions about how she felt, what it was like to wake up, and what she needed them to do for her. Every member of the Garzas' family and friends stood anxious to help and ready to do whatever was needed. Mr. Garza gave specific instructions to their visitors to not tire her out with endless questions. They were to allow her time to sleep, rest, and heal. He explained that, because she had been in a coma for such a long time, she had lost weight and would tire with even the smallest of effort. All this was true, but Gaby stayed awake as long as she could, bathing and reveling in the love of her family. Still exhausted from her all-night struggle to walk to the bathroom, Gaby was very tired and weak. After the trip home, a nap, some familiar food, and a few questions, she soon slept peacefully again.

Gaby had a challenging time getting through that first full day at home, because she wanted to fall back into her normal pattern, but could not. Gaby was so weak that she could only do a little of what she wanted. She had lost about twenty-five pounds and thought, *I am so skinny that my knees seem to be just bones covered with skin;* she weighed only eighty-three pounds. She couldn't sit up for long and had to go to the bathroom every fifteen minutes. She was very happy to see some of her school friends show up at her house, but she was in no shape to entertain them for long. Finally, Mr. Garza shooed everyone away to let her sleep.

NO POLKA DOTS

Beginning almost immediately, Gaby worked on learning to walk again and regain control of her hand and arm. Progress was slow and difficult. She worked hard on her tasks but soon tired, although day-by-day her strength and stamina returned. Soon she was spending most of her waking time sitting on the bench beside the dining table, talking with her mother.

One of the first things Gaby noticed when she arrived home was the polka-dot dress she was supposed to have worn to the graduation party on the day of the accident. It was still on its wire hanger suspended from a nail. The dress now represented something painful she wanted to forget.

"You need to take that dress and do something with it. I will never wear polka dots."

Gaby knew that her mom had worked very hard on sewing the dress; it fit perfectly and Gaby absolutely loved it. It was a shame to just discard it, but when Gaby saw it on the hanger after all that had happened on the day she should have worn it, she knew she could never wear the dress or polka dots. Gaby thought that maybe it had been the bad luck talisman heading the family into the accident. When she asked her mom to remove it and get rid of it, Sanjuanita was hurt. Gaby had to make a million excuses so that her mom would not make her wear it. Sanjuanita gave it away.

WHERE IS MY SMELL?

One day shortly after her arrival home, Gaby, gaining strength rapidly, sat at the table watching her mother work in the kitchen. She suddenly had a strong desire for one of her mother's best dishes. "Mom, do you know what I want to eat?"

"No, what do you want?"

"I want you to make me some *fideo*." Fideo is a Mexican version of spaghetti. It is a very savory, spicy dish that every cook in Mexico knows how to prepare, but that is never prepared in the same way in any two households. Fideo in Mexico is much like Bar B Que in Texas. Everyone has their own recipe and process. Most are very good, but all are a little different from all others. Gaby loved watching her mother prepare all the spices, grinding them together in the old-fashioned *metate* (a stone mortar and pestle). The tantalizing smell of the fresh spices was a feast in and of itself. Gaby savored and thoroughly enjoyed the odors of her mother's fideo spices. The pleasure of the spicy odors caused great anticipation. It was a wonderful homey smell that lasted through the meal and lingered in the kitchen long afterward.

Mrs. Garza finished her cleaning and began to grind and mix spices, preparing for the fideo. Gaby watched in great anticipation. After a while, Gaby realized she couldn't smell the spices being ground and mixed in the metate. She wondered why.

"Mother, are you sure the spices are fresh?"

"Oh, yes. Why do you ask?"

"Usually when you mix the spices, I can smell them from here. That is one of the greatest things about your fideo, the smell even before you cook it. But I can't smell the spices."

Mrs. Garza picked up the metate and took it to the table. She placed it under Gaby's face.

"Do you smell it now?"

Gaby breathed in the air above the mixture. "No, mama, I can't smell it."

With concern clearly showing on her face, Mrs. Garza brought perfume for Gaby to smell. Gaby could detect no odor.

"Go smell some Vicks."

Gaby struggled into the bathroom and found the Vicks and opened the jar, but still she could not detect an odor. Her mother dipped her finger in the Vicks and rubbed some around Gaby's mouth and nose. Still, Gaby could not smell it. Mrs. Garza brought a variety of things sweet and pungent, soft and strong, to see if Gaby could smell them. Gaby could not detect an odor from any of them. There seemed nothing to do, but now the incident of the anesthesiologist telling her the gas would smell like bubble-gum when, in fact, it had no odor suddenly made sense.

RETURN DOCTOR'S VISIT

Three days after realizing that she had lost her sense of smell, Gaby's mother took her to the same doctor who had released her from the hospital. Gaby wanted to see if the doctor believed her leg and arm would get better. For the most part, her arm and leg had remained weak and uncontrollable.

In what seemed to Gaby a feeble attempt at humor, the doctor brought Gaby's chart into the examination room, thumped it a couple of times, and asked, "Well, young lady, what is your problem?"

Gaby was not amused. In fact, she was insulted by this man she had had to work so hard to get away from. "I do not have a problem. I have a medical condition."

The doctor began talking to Gaby's mother in English about her. Gaby responded, "You need to talk to me. I am the patient, and my mother does not speak English."

"Take off your shoes." With some difficulty, Gaby complied.

The doctor scraped the bottom of her left foot. Her foot responded by jerking and pointing her toes downward. He then scraped the bottom of her right foot. Her toes reacted upward. Without saying more, the doctor walked out and did not return for a long while. Gaby sat nervously waiting for some answer. When the doctor finally returned, he had a nurse with him. The doctor did not explain that the normal reaction to scraping the bottom of one's foot is for the foot to point downward. The upward reaction in her right foot indicated damage in the area of the brain that controls the leg and foot. Any reaction is somewhat good. It indicates life. But an upward reflex is less than ideal.

"You need therapy. You need lots of therapy. Your whole right side is paralyzed, but it looks like it can be retrained."

"What kind of therapy? What do you mean?"

The doctor pulled a small hard rubber ball out of his right coat pocket. "Therapy like this. Put your right foot on the ball." Gaby picked her right leg up with her left hand and placed it on the ball. The doctor moved her foot in a small circle keeping the ball trapped underneath. "You have to learn to control your foot without assisting it, and you need a lot of therapy for your right hand and arm."

"What kind of therapy for my arm?"

Again the doctor responded with an example. He placed a pen in her right hand and a pad of paper in her lap. "Draw circles," he commanded. Gaby tried to draw a circle only to drop the pen. It clattered to the floor. "You see, you need help to get your strength and control back."

"How much?"

"How much therapy? A lot. We'll set you up on a schedule."

"No, how much?"

"Oh, do you mean how much will it cost?"

"Yes."

"About two-thousand dollars per session, but that is what it will take for you to get some use of your leg and arm back."

"I want to be normal, but we do not have that kind of money."

"Well, I don't know if you can get back to normal. But you can learn to use your paralyzed limbs again."

"If I do that with a ball I can get better?"

"Yes, you can get better. But that is not all you need."

"I don't want to just get better. I want to be normal." To her mother she said, "*Vamanos, Mama* (Let's go, Mama)." To the doctor she said, "We don't have the money."

Mrs. Garza helped Gaby to her feet and almost carried her all the way to their pickup moving as quickly as they could; all the while, the doctor and nurse tried to talk them into stopping and agreeing to the therapy. All the way home, Gaby could only think about the therapy and getting better. The doctor had given her an idea that she would start working on as soon as the slow-moving pickup got home.

As soon as they got home, Gaby got a small lemon from the foodstuffs in the kitchen and began working to gain control of her right leg and foot. She put the lemon on the floor under her foot, just like the doctor had shown her, and worked hard every day, many times per day, learning to control her right foot by keeping small objects trapped while moving her foot back and forth and in circles. Some ability to grasp objects had begun to return to her right hand. She asked for a pen and some notebook paper to exercise her right hand. She told all members of the family, especially her mother, to stop helping her do simple things. They were not allowed to help her get to the bathroom or shower. She decided that in order to get better faster, she had to struggle through alone. Several times over the next two weeks, she asked her father to get her more notebooks, and she sent her brothers for different things like spools, salt shakers, marbles, and soda bottles so that she could exercise her foot differently. Her determination to get better was paying off. She was gradually gaining movement, control, and strength. Now that she could see the progress in her physical well-being, and needing another challenge, her original summer project began weighing on her. If she could just get a little help, she was sure she could still complete seventh and eighth grade before school started.

20

Beginning Again

BACK FROM THE DEAD

On Monday morning, July 20, at seven thirty in the morning, I had been on the job less than an hour when the phone rang. Absently, I answered. "Cuellar Middle School. This is Hillrey Dufner. May I help you?"

What I heard next startled me, confused me, made me grateful to God, and jerked me to my feet.

"Well, Dufner, are we going to do this or not?" There was only one person in the world who simply called me "Dufner."

"Gaby? Gaby! Yes. Yes, we are going to do this. But how are you? Where are you? Are you able?"

"I'm waiting for you to pick me up. I thought you would be here at six thirty."

I ignored that I hadn't been to her house in over a month. "Well, we will get off to a late start today, but I'll be there in a few minutes to get you. Are you sure you are able to start back? I lost track of you and couldn't find out where you were."

"Yes, I can do it. But there is a little problem. Well...maybe two problems."

"What are they?"

"You will have to help me to your van. I can't walk too good yet. My right side is weak."

"That is no problem. I will do that. What is the other problem?"

"I might not be able to make the whole day. If I need you to, can you bring me home early?"

"Plan on it. You just let me know when. Is there anything else?"

"No. I just want to get started again. Do you think I can finish?" This was the first time I had ever heard even a shadow of doubt in Gaby. I was a little surprised, but actually relieved to see this very human and vulnerable side of her. I knew some adjustments would have to be made, I just had not had time to work out what we had to do differently. Gaby's expressed doubt gave me hope that she would accept some changes.

"Well, we have lost a lot of time. Let me study the situation and see what we need to do. I'll be at your house in a few minutes...and, Gaby?"

"Yes, Dr. Dufner?" There was a little apprehension in her voice. I had noticed earlier that she only used the doctor appendage to my name when she felt fear or great concern.

"This is exciting. You know, that you are well enough to start back. I have been very concerned about you. I couldn't get much information about you, and the information I got was not good. Welcome back."

"Good-bye, Dufner. Please come and get me."

"I will be there shortly. Good-bye."

The trip to Gaby's house was a long one, or so it seemed. I was so excited to see Gaby and get her started back on the path to her dream that I drove more slowly and carefully than usual to be sure I did not have an accident on the way to pick her up. When I finally came within sight of the Garza house, I could see Gaby leaning on the white door frame, holding the screen door open. She was waiting with her small sack lunch in her left hand.

REUNION

Twenty minutes after the call, I pulled my brown van into the Garzas' driveway, and a familiar scene was played out with only one major change. In the past, Gaby would be waiting inside the screen door, walk to the van, and climb in so we could leave for the day. This time I went to the door and supported Gaby as she walked unsteadily to the van. Gaby had little strength in her right side, so we had to figure out a way for her to climb into the passenger's seat using primarily her left hand and left leg. That model of Vanagon was pretty high off the ground, so there was not only a high first step, but the seat was taller than in most vehicles. It did present some difficulty for Gaby. Luckily, that model of Volkswagen van also had a handle just above and inside the passenger door to assist passengers getting in. It was located close to the top of the doorway. We decided that she could use her left hand to grasp the handle and lift herself up, negotiating her way into the seat. That bit of planning done and executed, we left much as we had for those short few days in the beginning of the summer.

On the way to the campus, I asked Gaby many questions about her accident and what had happened to her. She answered each question, but definitely gave the Reader's Digest version, leaving out many details. I helped her into the building and to her study room. I promised to begin the conversation later that day about what we would do to make up for the lost time.

THE NEW PLAN

Sometime in the middle of that first morning, I sketched a plan together. I walked into the office Gaby was using, and sat down beside the old table on top of which was stacked her materials. As we began talking, I told Gaby that I could not see any way for her to complete the two years of literature, science, and math she still needed in the short time we had left. I acknowledged that she was a strong-willed and committed student, but also that she was not strong of body and had lost more than six weeks to the accident.

I brought up the possibility of compromising the goal; instead of advancing all the way to the ninth grade, Gaby would advance to the eighth. Gaby immediately and emphatically rejected compromising the goal. She was adamant that completing both the seventh and eighth grades that summer was possible, and she renewed her commitment to completing the work. Her feelings were so strong that just the mention of backing off brought tears to her eyes and an angry edge to her voice. I tried calming her, telling her that there was another possibility, but that I would have to check it out first through the policies of the district and the TEA.

In the mid-afternoon of that first day back, Gaby requested to be taken home. She was tired and in some pain, but she also insisted on taking a literature book home to read. On the way, Gaby sat in the passenger's seat staring straight ahead, staring at the highway, saying nothing for most of the trip. Finally as we approached her home, she turned to face me and again brought up the subject of completing the work. Glancing her way, I saw that she had been crying. Tears streamed down both sides of her face and dripped unacknowledged from her chin. She begged me to allow her to complete the two grades. She promised that if all it took was for her to work harder, she would work harder; she would complete the task and achieve her goal, no matter what it took. She offered to take home more work and work late into the night. I told her that I would talk to her again the next day, but that she should do a little reading and get some rest.

At six thirty the next morning, Gaby was waiting at the door in good spirits. She and I went through the loading sequence we had devised the day before, and we were soon on our way. From the passenger's seat, she gave me a brief summary of what she had read the night before and asked a few questions based on her reading. She seemed to be ready for the day. I brought up the topic of skipping two grades. "I may have an idea that will help us develop a workable schedule. I have to call a few people back this morning then we can talk."

The color of the mood changed immediately from light and fresh to dark and heavy. Gaby seemed very apprehensive about leaving her future in someone else's hands; especially someone she did not know and could not talk to. The remainder of the ride to school was not unfriendly, just heavily silent. I knew she was preparing her arguments to convince me that she could finish all the work and finish it well. I suspected that she was way ahead of me as far as discovering possible avenues we could pursue, but she remained silent and respectful—somber.

Before I allowed her to go into the makeshift office, I emphasized to Gaby that her completion of both grades was second to her health. She could not be expected to work day and night and still make a full recovery. She needed time to do her physical therapy and rest. As I expected, Gaby objected, saying that she had already rested too much; she could do some of the physical therapy while she studied. It was pointless to continue arguing. I knew she would give herself no slack and that she would work to the point of exhaustion rather than give up. I also knew that proposing a rigid plan offering anything less than her goal would create a strong and unproductive emotional reaction, so I dropped the discussion for the moment, stating that I would come back later in the day.

I had to assure her that my mind was not set; that there was still a chance she could complete both grades. Satisfied, she went directly into her office and buried herself in academic work. She immediately started on a chapter test. She read passages and wrote answers for most of the morning. Around ten thirty that morning, she brought a section of completed assignments for me to look over. After reviewing the assignments and offering some feedback and additional assignments, I brought up the plan again.

"Gaby, I think I know a way you can have the time needed to complete both grades."

"What do I need to do?"

"Well, essentially you will have to fail a course in both the seventh and eighth grade."

"No! I have never failed a course, and I won't start now."

"Now that we have that out of the way, are you ready to listen?"

"Okay, I'll listen, but I already don't like this."

"The promotion requirements for the seventh and eighth grades both allow a student to pass onto the next grade while failing one core subject. As a practical matter, since the state tests math and reading, we cannot select either of them. I wouldn't anyway." Gaby nodded in agreement. "So I am suggesting that we push science to the end, both seventh- and eighth-grade science; we work on those courses last. If you complete the reading and math courses as well as pass your tests on all the courses but science, I can still certify that you have passed to the next grade, even if you don't complete science." Gaby was shaking her head and tears were welling up in her eyes. "Look, Gaby, I like your grit. I respect your effort, and I admire your tenacity. I have never had a student quite like you. I'm not sure you can't do just about everything, but the fact is we are running out of time. This way, you will complete the science courses if you can, but they won't stop you if you don't complete them. One of my concerns now is that you complete the eighth grade algebra course. No doubt you will whiz through the seventh grade math requirements, but the algebra course is not so easy, and math is not your strongest subject. The algebra course will require twice the effort of any other course you are now working to complete. In addition there is an end-of-the-year test that less than half of all eighth-graders passed last year. That test will be what recommends you to begin Algebra II, Algebra I honors, or just regular Algebra I in ninth grade."

Still holding her attention, I continued. "I think it is time now for you to trust me. You must work on the courses as I direct you. Trust me to guide you. You can meet your goal this way even if not every T is crossed. Remember from your social studies, that generals with vision occasionally enter a battle they know they will lose in order to bleed the enemy's resources. They do that so that later they can win the war over a weakened enemy. We're adopting a similar strategy. It's called losing a battle to win the war. We can fail a course to pass an entire grade."

The tears were on hold, but she still had concerns. "I want to be in honors classes. If I fail science, I probably won't be accepted into any honors class."

"Oh, that will not be a problem. I can help there."

"Even with failing grades?"

"Gaby, I will talk with the counselors and assistant principals that schedule students. They are friends of mine and will listen to your unique situation. Again I must ask you to put these worries aside and concentrate on your courses. Trust me to take care of the administrative details. I am really quite good at what little I do. I will not fail you. I will do as I promise."

Gaby nodded slowly, seeming to digest the information and wrestle with giving up some control. She sighed, and her face brightened as she made a difficult decision. She stood and opened the door. Turning to face me, she smiled and said, "I trust you. It is hard not being in control. It is hard not doing it all. Well, I guess I had better get back to the reading. I'm only about halfway through seventh grade." She was actually much further along than that.

"By the way, Gaby, there is a math teacher, a very good math teacher, who wants to help you with the algebra. Mrs. Valdez teaches eighth-grade Algebra on this campus. She has heard of you and wants to help. She will be back from her vacation and ready to begin on Monday. I think we should begin then." Gaby nodded her agreement and smiled. I admit that

I wondered at her giving up so easily, but perhaps she really did believe it was a good plan. We never spoke of it again. It was settled.

COMPLETING THE PLAN

Mrs. Valdez came to the campus to work with Gaby on Monday as promised, and Mrs. Sturgis began working with Gaby again. This time they worked on literature. As predicted, Gaby proved to be an able arithmetic student and shortly took the end-of-year test for seventh-grade math, passing it with ease. Shortly after, she passed tests in reading for the seventh and eighth grade proving she would be able to handle the State exams to be given the next spring. Her grades were not all A's, which did not please her, but she did refrain from dwelling on it.

While she worked on her courses, Gaby did reimburse the teachers by helping them with the task of straightening and decorating their rooms. I believe these tasks were physically and spiritually healing for her. Gaby's strength and coordination were returning quickly. There was no doubt in my mind that she would soon be strong enough to begin ninth grade.

FULFILLING THE DREAM

On the first day of the school year, Gaby was not yet finished with the eighth-grade algebra course. Mrs. Valdez felt that if Gaby was given a little more time, she could complete everything and pass the end-of-year exam. She asked to keep Gaby in her room the whole day for the first few days of school so that Gaby could concentrate all her school time on algebra, completing the course, and testing. Since Gaby had already passed every other course required for seventh and eighth grade except science, I agreed. The first and second day of school, Gaby studied in Mrs. Valdez' classroom, concentrating on her algebra and occasionally taking breaks to tutor other students. She took the algebra end-of-year test on the third day of the school year. She passed it with a score that equated to B. She was excited to be finished in time to begin the ninth grade. The question of science did not come up again.

When Mrs. Valdez related her score to me, I prepared a letter of certification to provide to the principal of the ninth-grade campus, and placed a copy in her permanent file. The letter was all that she needed to move into the ninth-grade.

During the summer, there had been a considerable amount of moving between campuses in the district to accommodate overcrowding at the high school. Ironically, the campus on which Gaby attended sixth grade was to be the new ninth-grade campus. So she returned to the Mary Hoge campus to begin high school.

In our final discussion before Gaby began ninth grade, I told her that she had to now prove herself to another set of teachers and administrators. I emphasized that she had done extraordinarily well under very trying circumstances even though she did not see that she had done anything unusual. I told her how proud I was of her and I promised to be at her beck and call if she needed me, but the execution of the rest of the plan was now up to her. Gaby gave me a tearful hug, as she was choked up too badly to talk. I commented that I had never seen her speechless before. That brought a smile.

Mrs. Peterson, the new ninth-grade assistant principal, accepted the letter and placed Gaby in honors classes. However, she would not place her in honors Algebra I for fear of overloading her. Gaby appealed to her unsuccessfully then called me. I called Mrs. Peterson, but she would not relent.

"Well, Mrs. Peterson, by the end of the first six weeks, she will convince you that you have made a mistake. When that happens, I want you to call me and eat crow." She laughed and agreed to call if it happened.

"If that happens," she promised, "I will move her to an honors class at the end of the first six weeks. This way she will have a chance to prove herself."

Gaby proved more than equal to the task. At the end of the first grading period, she had a hundred percent average in the regular Algebra I course and was complaining that the class was moving too slowly. Mrs. Peterson moved her to the honors section after calling me so I could feed her the promised blackbird stew. I was happy to say, "I told you so!"

At the end of each six-week grading period of her ninth-grade year, I quietly checked on Gaby's grades and progress. None of her teachers or administrators had concerns about her once they met her, especially if she was in a class with them. The fact that she did not attend seventh or eighth grade soon faded to become simply an interesting anecdote rather than a cause for alarm or diligence. She continued to improve physically and successfully completed the ninth grade, although she did faint a couple of times, bringing up discussions of possible long-term brain damage. Gaby was successful in explaining that the fainting was a malady she had suffered from long before the accident.

THE REST OF HIGH SCHOOL

Through her four years of high school, Gaby proved able to handle any and all academic challenges she faced. There seemed to be few lingering negative effects of her difficult summer between sixth and ninth grade.

Gaby babysat for my three young children many times throughout high school. She never had transportation, so I would pick her up and drop her off afterward. On the way to and from babysitting, we would discuss plans for getting her into college. Her biggest concern was her father, who felt that she must stay home with her mother. We talked at length about how she could convince her dad to allow her to go to college. Since her dad was expecting her to help the family financially instead of going to college, Gaby began searching for a way to help support her family financially while attending college. I never doubted for a moment that she could and would eventually solve the problem.

21

Graduation

G aby graduated from high school on time. She was sixteenth in her class of five hundred nineteen with a grade point average of 3.8 and many recommendations and honors intended to encourage her to attend college. I had no doubt that the stubborn child Gilberto and Sanjuanita Garza had raised would eventually best her father and go to college. I just wasn't sure how.

SCHOLARSHIP!!

During Gaby's senior year, she spent a lot of time applying to universities. She was offered many full scholarships, including one to Yale University. Their scholarships were offered to minorities in an effort to fill their 'equal opportunity quotas.' The offers disappeared once she informed the universities of her residential status as not yet a citizen of the United States. When the family crossed into the US, they had no idea they would have to wait fifteen years to obtain green cards. At the Senior Awards Ceremony, she was presented with a few small scholarships and received recognition in many categories.

She was unaware of her rankings and recognitions. Her counselor did not mention them to her. At the awards ceremony, she was asked to speak to her classmates in an effort to motivate them to move on to bigger and better things. One of the counselors thought her story was representative of strength, courage, and motivation, and worthy of being heard by the class. Gaby briefly talked about herself and some of the challenges she had overcome. She mentioned me in her speech, labeling me as her guardian angel. It was through flowing tears that she told the group not to ever give up on their dreams. She told her peers that there were many opportunities to further their education, if they would only look for them. Some of the tears ruining her make-up were shed because of the emotional release that came from talking about the difficult things she had struggled through to arrive at graduation, but they also came from the worry that all her dreams of college were coming to nothing. She felt as if her dreams were fading from possibility to memory. Her father didn't want her to go to college, and all the scholarships had been revoked. She was talking to herself as much as anyone in the audience, trying remain hopeful that she would be able to attend college, if not the coming year, soon. What should have been a time of celebration and anticipation was quickly becoming a moment of crisis that threatened her dreams. The reality was hitting her hard.

When the ceremony was over, she walked outside the gymnasium to wait for her father. She felt someone poking her shoulder and figured it was a classmate playing a trick. She ignored the poke the first and second time. The third time she felt the poke, she turned around in a state of frustration, and yelled, "What do you want?" She was very embarrassed when she found that the poking came not from one of her classmates, but an older gentleman she did not know. She walked away with her face feeling hot and turning red, even though the gentleman kept calling her name. She didn't know him and was embarrassed to face him after yelling at him. About a month into summer, Gaby received a letter from a Mr. Glen Roney inviting her to lunch. She threw the letter away, thinking that his proposal for lunch was inappropriate; she didn't know a Glen Roney and didn't have a clue why he wanted to have lunch with her. She threw away another letter from Glen Roney she received in July. Again in August, one week before college classes started, she received another letter from Glen Roney. This time the letter had a sentence that caught her eye "I want to help you further your education," it said. She immediately called and set up a date and time for their luncheon meeting.

At the luncheon, Glen Roney granted her a full scholarship for her first two years of college. Glen Roney became Gaby's new mentor and her other guardian angel. Mr. Roney encouraged her to obtain a bachelor's degree and promised to help her. He was as good as his word. He helped Gaby by giving her work at his bank and by helping with out-of-pocket expenses as well as tuition. Gaby had her dream. She earned money to help the family and went to college to earn a four-year degree, graduating with honors in 2001. There were many obstacles to her completing the four-year program, as there are for most attempting to gain a degree while working for funding, but Gaby would not be denied or defeated.

22

My Lesson

What did I learn? Many times at night, just before sleep takes over my mind and body, I have thought about what I learned from witnessing Gaby's commitment and courage. On those nights, floating between awake and asleep, I gradually began to realize that watching Gaby achieve meant witnessing a dream come true. Gaby saw very clearly what she wanted, and that vision became her goal. She did not allow pain, sorrow, disability, or those who wished to see her fail shake her belief that she could achieve anything she wanted. Gaby followed her dream through distressing and painful times that would have stopped most people. However, she innately knew that life is painful and distressing whether attempting the impossible or hiding and hoping the pain will go away. Gaby demonstrated that fighting to be a better and more successful person at least gives the suffering some purpose. Those who achieve endure the pain and discouragement, knowing that those feelings are part of the price they pay for the act of reaching to fulfill their dreams. Obstacles surmounted become landmarks of progress. Persons of Gaby's character and drive may fail, but if they do so, they fail bloodied and wiser from the attempt, not cravenly hiding from life. Knowledge gained in a failure informs another attempt. The act of attempting is alone a success.

Until I met Gaby and saw her amazing commitment, perseverance, vision, and high expectations of herself, I had dreams of writing a book, but never the commitment to try. I had allowed the demons of "I'll-begin-tomorrow," "I have nothing significant to say." and "Who-do-you-think-you-are?" to stop me short of putting one word on paper. Gaby taught me to reach for what I may not yet be able to touch, and to not give up climbing and reaching until I have it firmly in my grasp. Tomorrow is never here today, and today is all I can control. Tomorrow is always tomorrow. I started writing Gaby's story as a way to begin fulfilling *my* dreams. Without her example, I am not certain I would have ever started, and her example of perseverance encouraged me to complete the dream.

Looking at Gaby's life, a simple but profound truth is revealed: People who attempt the impossible are the same people who achieve the impossible.

Consider it all joy, my brethren, when you encounter various trials, knowing that the testing of your faith produces endurance. And let endurance have its perfect result, so that you may be perfect and complete, lacking in nothing.

James 1:2-4, New American Standard Bible

Epilogue

Gaby was married in 2003. In 2007 her first child, Gerardo, was born. He is a delightful boy she lovingly calls 'Peanut.' At the time of this publishing, Gaby is a loan specialist and manager for a large bank she helped found. Her next goal is to obtain a master's degree. She wants to become a teacher so she can have a direct impact on children who need someone to believe in them.

Even now Gaby cries easily. It would be natural to mistakenly see this tendency as a sign of weakness. It is not. The strong spirit, the determination, and the perseverance I saw demonstrated in her is very much alive and well.

God help the man or woman who doubts or attempts to stand in the way of Gaby's dreams. She will not be defeated. With her faith in God, the support of her family, and her indomitable spirit, she will always succeed, because she will focus everything she has toward her goals. I thank God often for allowing me to witness the extraordinary determination of this wonderful young lady. Without any intention of doing so, she became one of my heroes, and now, I hope, one of yours too.

Made in the USA
San Bernardino, CA
05 November 2013